Praise for this book

These angel messages were fi[rst sent out by] email list many people emailed me with their experiences, thoughts and ideas with the angels. Sometimes the email was a direct testimonial and others more of a personal note to me about how a particular message had resonated with them. The following testimonials are a selection of these messages; names have been changed in most cases.

'Words of beautiful loving kindness'

Aishling's Angel messages are full of insightful **wisdom and compassionate healing words** *that resonate in varying ways. Sometimes it's an answer to something I've been pondering, sometimes a gentle reminder of something already learned and not currently practicing, other days, it's a new insight or fresh way of looking at life and sometimes,* **it's words of beautiful loving kindness that I truly needed to hear that day.** *These messages are like a voice whispering to my deepest parts,* **a beautiful loving reminder that we are not alone,** *we are fully supported, guided and loved by the wise compassionate energy of Angels.*

Each message ensures I go about my day with a lighter heart, a positive reinforcement of love and something to ponder that lightens the mental load and lifts the soul.

Thank you Angels & Aishling, a true Earth Angel, much love **Caroline Kirk**

'Stunning words of wisdom, that are both sweet and poignant!' *I've noticed that I'm happier and lighter and when I'm facing something stressful, I know there is a source bigger than me, helping me. I'm tuning in more and more to my inner voice of wisdom and to the messages I'm receiving from my angels. It's truly beautiful and special to know that no matter what I'm going through in life, I'm not walking my path alone.* **Kate**

'A reminder to have faith, believe and stay in the vibration of love' *Aishling's angel messages have become part of my spiritual practice allowing me to connect even for just one minute, with the higher vibration and energy of angels.... especially on those days when I need a reminder to have faith, believe and stay in the vibration of love.* **Victoria**

Thank you very much for the angel messages, each and every one of them is unique and inspirational. I especially loved today's message **25. Light is an Illusion!** *Wow the depth and potential* *in the message is exceptional! Thank You! Love and Blessings* **Niamh**

The messages have brought me to a lovely peaceful place after years of heartbreak and despair. Thank you. xx **Dee**

'Resonated with me in a huge way' thank you so much for this particular message (81. We are in your belly), it has resonated with me in a huge way. I've been struggling with my self-image and am constantly battling my weight, pretty much my whole life. I have felt a breakthrough and I'm starting to feel a flicker of self-love & acceptance in my belly! **Emma** x x x

Beyond beautiful thank you ♥ **Caroline** [In response to 65. Be ready to forgive]

Your angel messages are helping me feel more confident and living without guilt shame or fear. Just knowing that I am truly loved means so much. The light forever shines and I am glad **I can rise above and overcome with all this help from above.** **Roberta**

'Yes OMG!' Laughed my butt off! Seriously, Yes omg! This is so true and so perfectly said. I definitely need to work on calming the mind chatter. **Alicia** [In response to No. 87 Solitude is not an option]

'Wonderful reminders'. Thank you ! Thank you! For your beautiful angel messages… They always inspire me and put me on the right path for my day… these wonderful reminders to call on the amazing and powerful support that is always ready to assist…
Phyllis

Thank you for your inspirational messages and kindness. I have found a new peace in my life.… I've become calmer in my heart and I'm able to detach from situations where I can't control.
Bridget x [In response to 88. Learn to control your feelings]

Thank you so much Aishling for the wonderful messages'. *My favourites are:* **Today See the Light** *- the day I read this message the light from the sun suddenly started shining through the office window where I work :-).* **Finding Peace in Your Own Heart** *- as I kiss my children goodnight while they sleep in their beds I can see the light beaming from their hearts which fills me with immense happiness.* **Animals are the Masters** *- only a few days ago my 5 year old son told me he had an angel and his name was Patch and that I had one too and mine was Shady (Patch and Shady were our beloved pets that have passed away). Thank you again* **Amber x**

'There is someone watching out for me'. These messages give me an overall sense of peace, belonging and being aware that on the next plane there is someone watching out for me. I know we make our own contributions to what happens in our lives but even if things aren't great at a particular time, I've realized more than ever that these glitches are a tiny spot in the overall "tapestry" of our lives, and someday it will all make sense. **Mary**

I am really grateful for your angel messages. I especially loved this one, given the circumstances in my life currently I really need positive thoughts. Thank you so much Keep up the good work!! Regards, **Ash** [In response to 35. When you feel sad, there are many angels around you]

'Sustains and energises me'. The message of constancy and presence that is part of every message, sustains and energises me. Thank you for your messages and work in the world. Love, light and peace **Cath**

Angels are with you

By

Aishling Mooney

Copyright © 2020 by
Aishling Mooney

All rights reserved. No part of this book may be reproduced in any form or by any electronic or mechanical means, including information storage and retrieval systems, without permission in writing from the publisher, except by reviewers, who may quote brief passages in a review.

ISBN²: 9798612821052

Cover Design: Elia Pirovano

Published by Amazon
Printed by Amazon

Email: hello@aishlingmooney.com

www.aishlingmooney.com

For Noah and Emily

Know that you are never alone;

An angel walks beside you today

Acknowledgements

I acknowledge with deep love and gratitude:

Everyone who took the time to write to me tell me how important these angels messages were to you. This encouraged me to put my ideas and these messages on paper.

My students and clients and everyone who I've ever worked with, you've taught me so much.

My Mam and Dad and my family and friends in Ireland for reminding me I always have a home and a place where I'm loved no matter what.

Deirdre, Niam and Gavin because you know me and support me like no one else ever can.

Martha, Marcia for your love and fearlessness, especially when I wanted to give up a million times over.

Melanie and Inga for your friendship and support, I'm truly grateful.

Noah and Emily for allowing me to be your Mammy, for hugs and kisses, movie nights and card games and for encouraging me the whole way through writing this book.

Elia for being there as my rock and my love supporting me through all the crazy ideas and projects, just because it makes it makes me happy. Thank you love.

The angels who have never left my side.

Contents

Welcome and getting started..2

How to use this book?...8

1. I am here 13

2. Open your eyes 15

3. Gentleness is our gift to you today.............................16

4. Solace will find you today 17

5. Peace is a state of mind and consciousness 18

6. Love is not a thing..19

7. Take a breath, and I am here......................................21

8. Take this moment...23

9. I am Jewish 24

10. Go to your belly..25

11. I am always there with you.......................................27

12. Your eyes are always open to us..............................28

13. Angels exist...30

14. Today see the light..32

15. Now is the moment...34

16. Love is the answer..36

17. Hate is contraction 37

18. You are safe today and every day.........................39

19. Watch out for your dreams....................................41

20. There are many angels available to you, today, right now 42

21. Sacred numerology is a language............................44

22. You have within you light......................................45

23. There is no need for further effort or striving for success 47

24. Every being is love and light 49

25. See through your angel's eyes................................51

26. There is a beauty in the world...............................53

27. Animals are masters on this planet at this time.............54

28. You will know your angel's name today..................56

29. Get grounded! 58

30. When is a good time to talk to your angels?...............60

31. Rest is the key to angel time..................................62

32. We only seek to guide you 64

33. Your loved ones never leave you.......................66

34. There is a beauty in your voice.........................68

35. When you feel sad, there are many angels around you .70

36. Grace is a quality that strives to enter your heart now ..72

37. Gratitude without emotion is useless..................74

38. Peace in your toes 76

39. Avail of the mysteries the animal kingdom holds for you 78

40. You are not who you think you are! 80

41. You ask and we answer.....................................82

42. We will send you earth angels 84

43. Peace is your aim 86

44. Today just give us one minute 88

45. 'Ain't no mountain high enough'......................89

46. Thy will be done..91

47. Healing is possible 93

48. This place is filled with angels..........................95

49. Your light is love..97

50. We are everywhere you are..99

51. There is love on this earth now............................... 100

52. All will be well.. 102

53. Instead of expectations have acceptance.................... 103

54. Everything is love 105

55. I see love and light... 106

56. I release control to God 108

57. We are all love... 110

58. You are a clear channel for divine messages................ 111

59. Rest!.. 113

60. I give up control 115

61. Peace is a state of mind.. 116

62. Give up the struggle... 117

63. Go in peace 119

64. Forgiveness is the key... 120

65. Be ready to forgive... 121

66. I love you, I forgive you.. 123

67. I see love today 125

68. Your desires are creating your reality......................... 126

69. You must take the first step 128

70. Embrace the child today 130

71. Ask and ye shall receive 132

72. Peace is a step towards love 134

73. You are on the path to peace 135

74. Our commitment to you is everlasting 137

75. How will you direct your love today? 138

76. We are in the quiet places 140

77. We have the map, let us show you the way 141

78. Go to your heart space 143

79. Trust your own sense of appreciation 145

80 A little knowledge of colour 147

81. We are in your belly 149

82. Love is my religion 151

83. We are waiting for you 153

84. Just one minute 154

85. Give yourself time 156

86. You are blinding light 157

87. Solitude is not an option 158

88. Learn to control your feelings 159

89. Match your feelings to the change you want to achieve. 160

90. Saturate your thoughts and ideas with love 162

91. It takes courage to listen to your heart 164

92. Practice makes perfect 166

93. All Masters were once Novices 168

94. Colours are nourishing for your soul 170

95. Symbols are signposts 172

96. There is a reason for everything 174

97. The reason you are here is to find love 176

98. It was always about love 178

99. You are on purpose 180

100. You are the milestone 182

Note from Aishling 184

101. The beginning of something, is also the end of something 186

102. All the world's a stage 188

103. Through Angel's Eyes 190

104. We agreed to walk with you through it all 192

105. You are God's light 194

106. Every second of the journey is rich with wisdom and beauty 196

107. Speak kindly to yourself 198

108. A simple flower, your greatest teacher 200

109. Just say YES! 202

110. Rest for renewal and regeneration 205

111. Bliss inside 208

112. Find your soul, and you will find peace 210

113. Find your soul, and you will find peace 212

114. You will reach a place of surrender 214

115. Happiness is an illusion 217

116. Rest a moment sweet angel 220

117. Get ready! Hero up! 222

118. The battle cry 224

119. There be dragons 226

120. Miracles are a fact of life 228

121. Remember you never walk alone; an angel walks beside you today 230

122. Go out into the forests, and you will find God 232

123. Nature is the fastest path to God 234

124. Feel the rain on your face 235

125. Can you hear your soul? 237

126. Just STOP and you will arrive at your destination ... 239

About Aishling 243

My story 245

What's next? 252

Book Bonuses & Support 254

Your Angel Notes 255

Introduction

Welcome and getting started

One morning I woke from a dream, and I heard these words... it was a male voice, and he said;

'Did you tell them I am coming?' He said to the wind.

'Yes! But they do not notice me on their faces anymore...'

These first two short lines went around and around in my head for a few days. The voice came from inside me, although it sounded male.

I didn't get the rest of the message just these two lines. Finally, I made some time and sat down at my computer and wrote them into a word doc. As soon as I wrote these two lines, I could hear the next two lines and so on.

I began to sit every day for a short period in the mornings and just write. The words flowed through me one sentence at a time. I couldn't see ahead, I would always only receive the next one or two sentences and nothing else until I got that down on paper, then the next piece would be revealed.

I wrote as if from dictation.

As more messages began to form on paper, I realized that this series of messages would contain every piece of angel wisdom that I had learned and absorbed over many years working with my angels and guides. I also knew that this was an opportunity to share it all in one place.

I decided to release the angel messages as a daily email series and asked my community for their thoughts, feedback, favourites and testimonials. Over the course of about a year, more than one thousand people from all over the world, accessed the daily angel messages and I received many emails filled with words of kindness, thanks and appreciation. The overall feedback was that the messages were helpful, comforting and healing for those that read them.

Some felt the messages really helped and supported them through particular issues they were struggling with. Others found they gained a deeper connection to their angels and their own intuition.

Then I got busy and the messages slowed down until I eventually stopped writing them and emailing them. I also had a visitation from Archangel Metatron my main angel guide and he explained that they didn't need to be written in a hurry or in one sitting.

I became busy building my online spiritual business. As it began to grow I was asked how I did it by other spiritual practitioners and healers. So I began to teach, everything I knew about creating and growing a successful spiritual business.

I became a mentor to Lightworkers and I helped a lot of people get their businesses up off the ground in my programmes and online community spaces. But my heart always called me back to this book and these messages. I noticed that even though my spiritual business mentoring was successful, a large portion of my community and email list was for the angel messages.

It took nearly five years for me to come back to the messages and decide to give them my full focus and finally get them into this book that you're holding in your hands.

The nudge to write again didn't come wrapped in a pretty parcel this time or an angels voice in my ear but instead more like a big crashing bang. One night at 2am I found myself awake having difficulty breathing. I thought I was having a heart attack, later I learned it was experiencing severe anxiety and panic attacks.

I had been working too hard for too long. The result was severe anxiety. My body physically reacted every time I approached my computer… there was a sense of dread and anxiety. My heart literally flipped and started beating harder and I struggled to breathe.

I had to take a step back from my online business completely for six weeks to completely recover.

I wrote about the whole experience in a blog post called Breakdown to breakthrough.

One of the main things that restored my health was listening to my own angel meditations that I had recorded over the past ten years working with angels. I did all of the meditations and I simply began to feel better.

Although I still worked with angels in my personal life every day, in my spiritual business, I spent less than half my time talking about angels and the rest talking business.

Talking and teaching about business just wasn't satisfying me on a soul level anymore. I knew that I needed to get back to my angel work and share these angel messages.

In my recovery to full health again I decided to focus on my love of working with the angelic realms and showing whoever wanted to know, how to connect with them in every area of their life.

To begin I re-opened those emails and began to read again the testimonials and messages from people all over the world. I gathered them all into more than fifteen pages of testimonials. I cried as I read words of gratitude and love and I could see that the messages had already helped so many people.

I knew it was time to get this book completed and into your hands. I hope it helps you to connect with your angels at a deeper level.

My favourite angel message is this one below:

'Remember you are not alone, an angel walks beside you today.'

All my love

Aishling xxx

P.s. I've created a bonus page for you at www.aishlingmooney.com/bookbonus where you can access bonuses to support you in accessing the angelic realms and your journey with this book.

P.p.s. To contact us or let us know how these angel messages have helped you in your life please drop us a line at hello@aishlingmooney.com

We love to hear from you!

How to use this book?

This book covers everything you've ever wanted to know about angels. It's a journey walking alongside your angels every day. You can read a message a day or randomly open the book at whatever page feels appropriate.

I'd recommend that you read it through once, one message at a time and even possibly one per day, as the messages build on each other. Or you can use the book as an oracle and randomly open it to give you guidance and support with any area of your life. But please feel free to use it in whatever way supports you best right now.

If you are using it as an oracle…

Sit quietly, take a deep breath and ask your angels for their support and love. If you have a particular question, you can pour out your heart as if you were sitting with a really good friend.

Then open the page and read through the message for that day. Take a moment to just think about what's coming through in the message.

Sometimes it may not be immediately obvious and the words may seem to have nothing to do with your question or your issue. However, as I often tell my clients, healing can be beneath the words, it can be in the energy that's literally between the lines.

Just allow the message to work and possibly offer you healing throughout the day.

Just a heads up there are some messages that even as I channelled them I didn't feel comfortable or even agree with and paused before writing them down. However, I saw that with a little contemplation and asking myself questions about the buttons being pushed and why it was uncomfortable, I was able to see things from a different perspective.

My advice is to try it, read the book and see how it changes your vibration. I notice that I just feel better when I spend some time every day working with angels even if that's only for a few minutes.

What I do know after working with angels for over 20 years is that your angels are there right beside you now *and* they want to help you. In fact that's the main message of this book from angel message **No.121 'Remember you are never alone, an Angel walks beside you today'**

Your angels are responding to you before you even ask a question. There is no time lapse between when you ask a question and they respond. They are listening to you all the time and speaking with you all the time. This book will help you hear that inner voice more loudly and it can begin to guide you every single day.

Who is the voice in the messages?

During the period when I wrote the angel messages I was working mainly with my angel guide Archangel Metatron. However, I have also worked with many different angels, ascended masters, goddess and light energies over many years. I shared a lot of what I learned through my courses and programmes including the Transform with Angels and Mastery with Metatron and now in Your Angel Circle Membership Community.

Sometimes the voice in the messages says 'I' and sometimes it says 'we'. I feel the book was directed by Metatron but holds the collective energy of many angels and beings of love.

My feeling is that the really important thing about these messages is *how* they make you feel and not what angelic being gave them to us.

In the messages I've also used the word God, please replace that with whatever works for you: Universal Spirit, Great Mystery, Holy Mother or Father, Goddess, Love.

I personally interchange the word God with Love, and I often replace he with she or vice versa. Please do whatever feels good for you, whether you identify with male or female or neither I know you can identify with this desire to experience, give and receive love. Aren't we all just spiritual beings having a physical experience on earth? As Marianne Williamson says in her book; return to Love: *"Love is to people what water is to plants."*

I feel these messages are for everyone regardless of religious or spiritual beliefs and practices.

Your Angel Messages

1. I am here

I woke this morning from a dream, and I heard these words... it was a male voice, and he said;

'Did you tell them I am coming?' He said to the wind.

'Yes! But they do not notice me on their faces anymore.'

'Did you tell them I am coming?' He said to the moon and the stars.

'Yes! But they do not look up at me in the night time.'

'Did you tell them I am coming?' He said to the ocean.

'Yes! But they do not come to me for refreshment anymore.'

They have asked for me

I am here

But they cannot see me

Today my beautiful angels go out into nature and listen to her sweet song as she communicates with you and tells you stories of ancient beings that love you and walk with you. You are loved beyond reason, you are loved beyond doubt.

Get out of your homes, go outside and see me, feel me and know that I am God.

Come to me today.

2. Open your eyes

We are waiting, you have called, and we have answered. We are here.

There is nowhere that we cannot go.

You have called, and we have answered.

Now you must open your ears and open your eyes to see us clearly.

Your inner eyes and inner ears also, these are the real places that can see us.

Open your hearts and minds and allow us in.

Be assured: you have called, and we have answered

We are here with you now!

3. Gentleness is our gift to you today

There is nothing that cannot benefit from this now in your life.

Seek to be gentle with yourself and your mind and heart. Lead with gentleness, open doors with gentleness.

We treat you so gently, as if you were a precious newborn child. We cradle you in our presence and comfort you, holding you close to our hearts.

You are safe, and you are loved.

Be gentle with yourself today.

4. Solace will find you today

There is a gentle place, a space behind your eyes. If you close your eyes and go there, you will find a gentleness and emptiness that is so full of life, that you can fall into and float in its beauty.

This is God's heart, and it's right there behind your eyes. Look into that place, and you will find us.

You will find me there today.

Breathe, focus with gentleness, and you will find me there.

Do not strain, there is no effort.

It is gentleness, the opposite of what you have already learned.

You have learned this from man.

Learn this from me now.

Be gentle with yourself, look behind your eyes and you will find me there, and I am you.

5. Peace is a state of mind and consciousness

There is nowhere I cannot go. I am within you right now. You have called me, and I have answered you, even before you made the call.

The call is already answered.

I am here right beside you, before you even think the thought or utter the words, that you have need of me.

I have never left you.

I cannot ever leave you.

It is you who chooses to leave me.

And then there is darkness.

It is a choice you can make every moment of every day.

Choose peace and choose me.

I am right here beside you.

I walk with you today and every day.

You are never alone.

6. Love is not a thing

Love is not a thing. Love is not a commodity that you can buy and sell, although you try to all the time.

It is funny for me to watch you try to find it out *there*.

Love is within you.

There is no secret key to access it.

You are love.

If you could see the purity that I see when I look at you.

If you could see your own light shining, you would be blinded by that light.

If you could open yourself to the light in others and in the world around you, you would walk around bathed in brightness, even on the darkest night, cloudiest morning or rainiest day.

I am with you, and I am love.

I am your brother and your sister.

We are the same.

You are love.

You are loved.

Peace be with you, my sweet child and brother.

7. Take a breath, and I am here

Your breath is the gateway, of that there is no doubt.

It is called prana or life force in yoga.

You are breathing in life force with every breath that you take today.

How is your breathing?

Check-in on it right now and talk to me.

How is your breathing?

Can you deepen it?

Can you make it faster and slower?

Right now?

How does it make you feel?

You can breathe in life force and then more life force, whenever you need it in your life.

Breathing in life force brings you back to God.

Breathing in life force brings you back to me.

Breathing in life force brings you back to you and love.

Today just breathe, every hour bring your focus here and notice how you are breathing.

Play with this, have fun.

You are so beautiful.

8. Take this moment

There is a moment in every day when you will know that I am here.

Take *this* moment...

Notice your body. Now the area outside your body. Now the area inside your body.

That space, that emptiness is me.

Take a breath, breathe in some life force.

Now notice your body, go outside, go inside.

Seek to sense that tangible nothingness that is new and yet you've always known it.

You can sense this is who you really are, that which inhabits this body but is not this body.

9. I am Jewish

I am Jewish, I am Muslim, I am Christian.

I am all of you and none of you.

I am everywhere and nowhere.

I am inside you and around you, and you are too.

Notice your breath as you read these words.

Do you recognise the truth in them?

I am you and you are me.

I am love and I am you.

10. Go to your belly

There is a fire there in your belly.

It is the place that will teach you the most, about your feelings and emotions.

These are a vehicle to help you steer through this life.

They are an access point to me, to you, to discover what I have designed for you.

You are called to action daily in my service.

Your belly and your gut is the place from where I call to you.

You will hear my voice.

It is a tug, a knot an instinctual pull of recognition as you see someone or something that is important on your path.

Someone or something that you need to interact with.

Promise me you will take some time today, to bring your attention back down into your belly.

Go to your belly now and put aside your negative tirade of abuse, that you may have been directing there daily.

Instead, stop today and just go there.

Go there and find the fire within you.

I promise you it is there.

I put it there and I am you.

I know what you need and I know what's the next step for you.

I will talk to you constantly.

Do not drown out my voice with excesses.

Do not distract yourself today with negative thoughts and ideas about how your belly should and could be.

Instead, just love your belly as much as you can today.

And actively search for the fire that I promise you is there.

11. I am always there with you

There is a moment in every day when you will recognise me, and you will sense me and hold me in your breath and your mind.

I am always there with you.

But most of the time you will ignore me.

But it is you that has called for me.

I have answered you.

I am here now.

I am with you walking by your side.

I am you and I can never leave you now.

Take this moment and make it more, by just expecting it and knowing that it is real.

As you come to realise that I am here with you, regardless of how your life is appearing to happen to you. I have come to show you the way that you taught me.

I am here now in this moment.

You will see me soon.

12. Your eyes are always open to us

Opening your eyes is the strangest thing for us to see.

Your eyes are always open to us.

You are a spirit in this body, and although the body needs to sleep and recuperate and regenerate every day, your spirit has no need to sleep.

Your eyes are always open, you are always learning and seeing the beauty of the world around you.

There is a part of you, the real part, the true part, that is living your time here on this planet as a spirit. You never sleep, every moment counts as a point of learning and movement.

We are soaking up this experience of life that you are having. It is beautiful.

You are stunning, and you love it here. Whatever is happening to you in your life is an external experience.

It's happening to your body. And your spirit, the silent witness is recording these experiences moment by moment.

Your spirit is detached and an observer of your journey here.

The key to bringing beauty back, is to connect with this observer on a daily basis.

Ask that part of you that is love that is pure spirit;

What it has learned today? What has been recorded? What can be achieved today?

We are talking about separation, to help you find the many parts of your being, so you can eventually integrate this understanding and BE in a new way.

There is no separation.

There is only you and you are love. I am you and you are me.

However for today, just imagine that you have a witness inside of you, observing your life and see through their eyes what is happening and all that you have learned.

13. Angels exist

Angels exist and you are one.

There is an angel that walks by your side.

This does not make us different.

This does not make one better than the other or more powerful.

We do not have a body; we are fully integrated children of God.

We know what our mission is and our purpose.

We exist to serve God, we exist to serve you.

You are God, you are the light, and we are you.

Each of you has been assigned many angels that will appear and disappear throughout your life.

We will come when you have asked us to.

It is written in your sacred contract.

You asked us, and we agreed to be your angels and to walk with you through life's lessons and learning's.

Sometimes we will take on human form or even be part of the people in your life that cause you the most pain.

This suffering that you perceive is a tool for learning and growing.

You can move through anything.

You are powerful, and we are here to help you to realise that power and to remember who you are.

There is a light inside of you that can never go out.

There is a beauty that is visible to us, that takes our breath away each and every moment of every day.

You have chosen this path and we have agreed to walk with you.

We will serve as your guide to show you which way to turn and sidetrack and dance and skip and jump until you can do it by yourself.

You have called for us and we have come.

From now we will become more visible to you.

Open your eyes and see the world differently.

You are safe, we love you.

You have company on the journey.

14. Today see the light

The light is irresistible to a moth

There is a light that is inside you, and around you, that is like a magnet for your focus and consciousness.

Think about a time when you watched the flames of a fire, and you became lost in the beauty of the moment and those flames.

Do you remember what it felt like?

There was emptiness.

You didn't have to go anywhere or do anything, you may have lost time.

The lights that are visible to your physical eyes on the first level are to awaken you to us.

To awaken you to the light within you.

Today notice the light around you, as the sun shines in through the window, even if only for a short time today.

Notice the lights and the shadows and in the evening, look at the lights in the sky. See the moon and the stars and understand that, as you gaze in awe at the beauty of the galaxies and the light that fills your sky, you are admiring the light that is within you.

Take the light that is within you, all that you can see and then multiply that by 100 times. We have told you it is blinding; it is so beautiful, that when you see it, you will not need these physical eyes any longer.

Today see the light.

15. Now is the moment

In every moment, there is a chance to grow and expand.

We give you these opportunities every day.

The choices are sitting still, go backwards or move forward.

It seems easy.

Yet you constantly choose to go backwards.

It's a habit.

And one you must consider carefully and become conscious of, even if you don't know how or fully believe us.

Accept that there will be many opportunities today, to break free from oppression, anxiety and pain.

Just accept this and be open to noticing them.

They are the tiny moments of peace, the in-between moments when you find yourself thinking of nothing.

The pause in-between thoughts and breaths.

You can always find us in the breath.

Staying in pain is a choice.

There will always be a moment today and every day when there is no pain.

Be open to finding that moment today.

16. Love is the answer

There is a thing you call love.

There is a song or two on the subject you will agree.

You will do many things for love.

You will make changes in your life based on how you think you love.

There is a choice today to see love differently.

To find a kind of peace in your relationships and your desires.

So you never fear to lose another again.

The answer lies in your own heart.

Sit quietly today and listen to the silent sound of love inside of you as it fills every part of your heart and then your being.

You *are* the love inside you.

Even if you don't believe it's true yet, today just take our word for it.

17. Hate is contraction

The opposite of love and expansion

There is no reason to hate, but there is a place of displacement where you may feel that you need to express this emotion.

The truth is that it isn't the truth!

It's a complete illusion.

There is an opportunity to feel and act with love in every moment.

There is also the illusion that you can be hateful.

You can act hateful, but it can never tarnish your heart in any way.

Your true essence is always to love no matter what you do.

Karma redresses the balance between love and hate-filled actions.

There will always be balance.

As you act with love, love will be returned to you many times over.

As you act with hate, hate will be returned to you many times over.

But YOU will never be diminished or less than love.

18. You are safe today and every day

We know sometimes you feel sad or upset with life and you worry about every little and big thing that you think is happening to you.

Understand that it is happening for you!

Beware of your thoughts and crystallise your aims with as much control as you can muster.

What you focus on for too long will come about.

This is good news if it's something that you want.

This is bad news if you focus and constantly think about something you do not want.

The really good news is that you have a choice today, right now how and what to think.

Ok, your mind may whirl and wander down laneways and pathways that don't serve you.

But if you have a clear vision of what you want, then you can backtrack. You can get back on track like a traveller reading a map who is lost for a moment.

You are always safe, even when you take diversions.

We love it when you listen to us as we whisper in your ear today:

'This way, this way'.

You are never alone, and we walk beside you wherever you choose to wander.

19. Watch out for your dreams

We come to whisper to you in the night.

As you sleep and are relaxed, we can finally penetrate your ego mind and the noise and busyness of your day.

We leave little messages for you within your dreams and positive feelings for you when you wake.

Sometimes you hear our voices in your ear and as you come back to the world, we whisper your name and say:

'I love you, sweetheart.'

Take note of your dreams!

20. There are many angels available to you, today, right now

There's one for every category of help that you have need of.

'Angels find me a parking space!' we love that one.

Equally, we love 'Angels find me a new relationship that serves my highest good!' and 'Angels I'm lost! Help me find my way!' and even 'Angel I've lost my lipstick, where is it please!'

All requests are equal to us.

It's you who give each thing its own weight and value.

Today just ask for what you want and assume it's easy for us to bring it to you.

If you 'think' it's a difficult thing to achieve, a new house, job, relationship, etc... instead think about how you would feel, if you asked us to help you find your keys and how easy that would be.

Apply the same energy you feel when things are easy and too tasks you think are difficult.

In other words

1. Tell us what you want.

2. Think: That's EASY!

3. Feel: That's EASY!

Watch what happens............

21. Sacred numerology is a language

We'll use numbers to communicate with you. Many of you already know this and practice understanding it as so.

Many of you feel a tingle when you see 11:11 or 101 or 22:33 or 777.

These recurring numbers all carry a different value and message within them.

Numbers that you notice like this are signs from us that we've heard you and that we're listening. We are saying that we love you and that your prayers are being answered.

Notice the numbers on the clock today, on the car registration in front of you, on that billboard, in that overheard conversation or on that scrap of paper that lands at your feet.

Look for us today in numbers, surrounding you as we do with love and light.

You are beautiful! 11:11

22. You have within you light

There is a God inside you that is more powerful than you will ever admit to yourself or anyone else.

We can see this God shining, this being of light.

We can see the glass house of illusion and mirrors that surround this light.

The light you're currently emitting is artificial and man-made.

It has been created by you, because you thought you needed it to survive on this planet.

You have within you light.

Today, recognize that the glass is not real; that the real you is inside of you, behind the glass.

As you look in the mirror today, look into your own eyes.

Take more time than you usually would and see yourself there.

Call out to your soul.

Tell your soul that you can see it.

Do this often throughout the day. Whenever you pass a mirror or glass or catch sight of your reflection, look into your own eyes and say' I see you, I know you're in there'

This simple exercise has the ability to stir an ancient wise and wonderful being within you that has been quietly waiting for you to notice and remember that there is light inside you.

If you could only see what we do, this would be so much easier.

Today call out to your soul and let it know that you can see.

23. There is no need for further effort or striving for success

There are concepts and ideas that are difficult to assimilate and learn.

Nothing that we talk to you about is hard.

Remember who you are.

Remember why you're here.

Realise your full potential.

Return to love and return to power.

It is simple, and it is easy.

Yet you will continue to make it difficult for yourself.

Your ego wants it to be difficult.

You have trained yourself to think that this life has to be difficult.

You must work hard.

You need to make efforts to succeed.

Today let it all go.

Take our word for it.

You are already all you seek to be.

There is no need for further effort or striving for success.

There is only a need for stillness and in that stillness, an acceptance that you are love and that is all you need today and every day.

24. Every being is love and light

Look into the eyes of strangers.

Look into the eyes of animals that you meet today.

Look into their eyes and see the beauty of the souls that fill this planet.

See the beings of light that you walk with and that pass you by.

Use our eyes today *and* your imagination.

Imagine that everyone you meet has a bright shining light emitting from their heart centre. All living beings have this light. Refuse to be drawn into the ego's world of differences and anger and criticisms.

It may be easier to see this light, to begin with, in those you love

With careful and consistent practice you will be able to see this light in all beings regardless of how you see them act in the world.

You will begin to see true love in all its forms within each and every one of you

25. See through your angel's eyes

There is an idea that light comes from a point and flows out from this point.

We can see only light and colour.

When we look through your eyes, everything becomes grey.

To refine your sight, to get back this gift for seeing completely; Think about coming out of a movie theatre and how everything seems to shine a bit brighter.

Think about a time in your life when you felt at one with the day, or the environment you were in or people you were with. When it all just felt perfect and actually looked different, brighter.

This is how it can be all the time.

For now, you are beginning to train yourself to see completely again, as you did when you were a child.

You can regain this sight. We will give you the tools. For now, assume you already can see perfectly and know that you will begin to get glimmers of this new world of light and colour that is opening itself to you again.

26. There is a beauty in the world

There is a beauty in the world which you haven't experienced yet completely.

This beauty comes with a feeling or a sensation that's physical and emotional. You can sense it within you as you see a beautiful sunset or experience the birth of your child. That feeling of beauty that comes in these moments is a gateway and a key to God's treasures.

This key has the potential to unlock new levels of consciousness and personal and spiritual development within you.

Take our word for it.

Today as you go about your day, seek out beautiful things in your life, in the people that you meet and the things that are in your environment. Your favourite pen, a flower, a child's eyes, the shining soul of a dog or cat.

Expect to see beauty and know that recognising this is bringing you closer to God.

27. Animals are masters on this planet at this time

The consciousness of animals is so close to God. If you would just spend some time with them today and receive their messages of love and beauty and how the soul should live, your life would be transformed.

Find the animals on your planet seek out these master beings and spend time with them.

Go to the countryside, talk to the birds and watch the insects closely. Each animal has a specific blueprint and master messages encoded into its being, and it lives that message every single second or every day.

Treat these animals as the ancient and wise beings they are.

Be reverent towards them, be humbled and above all be kind.

Their greatest gift to you is to allow you to believe you have power over them.

They are the ones in control of their destiny.

They have chosen you to teach, while they are here in physical form.

The animals that surround you in your life are angels in physical form.

Angels walk beside you today.

Feel blessed that your world contains animals.

28. You will know your angel's name today

Start with your guardian angel.

Take a breathe and plant your feet firmly on the ground.

You are peaceful.

You are safe.

Use your imagination and see an angel standing in front of you.

See this angel is every detail.

Use your imagination and imagine what they would look like.

Notice the colour of their eyes, their hair and their clothes. Do they have wings? What is their predominant colour? Are they big or small?

This is your guardian angel

What is their name?

Ask, and ye shall receive.

It may come directly into your consciousness right now, or it may come later.

For now be open to receive

Know that you have an angel walking beside you today. They are with you in every single breath you have taken, since you choose to manifest in a physical form on this planet.

Today walk with your guardian angel.

There's a FREE Guardian Angel Meditation to support you with this exercise at:

www.aishlingmooney.com/bookbonus

29. Get grounded!

Planting your feet on the ground and using your breath to focus your mind even if that is only for a moment, is one of the best things that you can do for yourself today.

You are a spiritual being of light that has chosen to BE in this physical body during this lifetime.

You have chosen this and everything that is going on in your life.

It may be hard to hear this, especially if you perceive things to be going badly.

We tell you this to empower you, to show you that you have the power to choose how you are going to react from this moment on, to this lifetime and everyone in it.

You can take back your power and realise that you are a being of pure light and of God's loving energy. We see you so purely and beautifully, that it fills our hearts and makes us shine brighter so that you can see us.

Seeing orbs is a sign that we are showing you our love.

As we show you our love and you start to see us, you start to love us as well.

First it's unconscious, then it's obvious.

You start to feel good just by recognising that we exist. Your scientists are starting to see the benefits of love, to your health and well-being.

Feeling loved will help you to feel grounded.

Focus on your feet.

Breathe.

Allow yourself to see our love for you today.

Watch out for flashing lights and coloured orbs as you go about your day.

We love you so much my sweetest heart.

30. When is a good time to talk to your angels?

Well, we would like to say anytime, and while that is true on some level, there are times that you are more open to hearing and seeing us.

Bringing yourself into a place of relaxation and peace can help you to communicate with us more clearly.

Recognising the beauty that surrounds you, seeing love and light in other beings and breathing and placing your feet flat on the floor. These all help throughout your day to create an environment where you can hear and see us more clearly.

In truth we are always communicating with you, we never stop talking, whispering, shouting, sending you signs and messages through others including your environment.

Whether you can hear us or not is to a large extent up to you.

Creating any sort of spiritual practice where you acknowledge that this is your angel time will really help. This can be as little as three minutes a day, or for as long as you want. With continuous practice, it will become easier to hear us and for us to communicate with you.

You can use any type of meditation practice for your angel time. Also regular respite and rest can bring you into a place where we can enter your mind and talk to you.

Soon you will be speaking to us as if we are old friends. You'll recognise and learn to feel, hear and sense our presence around you. You'll turn to us in your angel time and ask for guidance.

Your angel time begins with as little as three minutes and then grows as you do in confidence and love.

Today realise that we're walking with you and talking to you all the time.

31. Rest is the key to angel time

Angel time or God time or spiritual holiday, whatever name you wish to call it, can be one of the most amazing gifts that you give yourself and your family, and the people you share your life with.

Regular breaks and check in times will help you to get clear, become more confident and give you a sense of security as you live your life.

When you start to truly believe that you have a guide walking with you, a true friend and confidant that always has your best interests at heart, your life will get easier.

You will know that when you're unsure, uncertain and feeling low that you just need some angel time. You just need to draw back into your space that you've created to share with your angels.

We'll be there for you.

We're always there for you.

We're just waiting for you to realise this and then we can really start in earnest to help each other.

Take regular rests in your day, close your eyes often, sit in stillness, breathe and do things consciously.

Even reading these messages every day is helping you to regain yourself and remember your true soul potential.

Today have a break!

There's a FREE Guardian Angel Meditation to support you with this exercise at:

www.aishlingmooney.com/bookbonus

32. We only seek to guide you

There is a tone we use to speak to you.

You recognise this tone now.

It comes with repetition and by listening to these messages every day.

And by taking these words into your heart, we have an opportunity to come closer to you.

The tone is obvious, it is the tone of love, deep compassion and understanding and absolute awe at your beauty and your presence and your light in this world

We are here to support you, to love you, to show you the way forward.

To show you the best way for you.

We only seek to guide you to the best possible path and solutions for you, at this moment in your life.

You have called for us to be here and we are here.

All you need to do now is open up to our messages and to these words, and to this love, to this voice inside of you.

We love you dear sweet child

33. Your loved ones never leave you

Your loved ones never leave you, even though there may come a time when they leave their body.

This physical body does not live on its own; it requires a soul to exist at all.

Like an empty house, which was once vibrant and beautiful because people lived there, the building becomes derelict from lack of use; this is the same for your body.

It is only a house that is beautiful and useful for as long as you need it, your loved ones do not need a body when they pass over. They have chosen to move on in their path, in their life.

But just because they don't have a body, does not mean that they are not here with you, every single step of your journey.

We are all connected, we are all the same. With spirit there is no separation of your soul.

There is no separation, we are one.

Your loved ones can come to your aid immediately when you call them, even if they are not in a physical body at this moment in time,

Their love still has the same intensity, indeed its intensity increases because they are no longer encumbered with the same past issues, behaviours and patterns, they had while walking on this earth. They are free right now.

Believe us, this is the truth.

There is no death.

Take solace in this great news today.

We love you.

34. There is a beauty in your voice

When you sing, when you dance, when you use your voice to contact us, we sing with you.

We love to hear you use your voice clearly and directly to create whatever you wish to manifest in this life, at the moment.

There is something to be said for claiming and for commanding, whatever it is that you want.

You can use your voice to claim your goodness in the universe. Your voice is one of the most valuable tools you have, in manifesting everything you could ever wish for.

Think about what you want and then speak it.

You are using your voice, all of the time to manifest the life that you are living now.

Begin to become aware of the words that you speak and also the words that you ingest from the radio, television, the internet and from the people around you.

The words alone don't have power, it is the tone behind these words that count.

When you wish to manifest something, beware of the tone you use.

If you could see the colours and the darkness of anger and the power of angry words, you would seek to fill your words with love.

Try this today, speak with love, it doesn't actually matter what the words are.

It is the power of emotion, that is behind the words and the way in which the words are delivered this is important.

Speak kindly to your fellow human.

Speak kindly to yourself.

Speak kindly and with love today.

35. When you feel sad, there are many angels around you

We are actually drawn like a magnet to this energy.

Our purpose is to help you no matter what.

We are programmed by God to help you.

Whenever there is sadness, we are there with you.

The deeper your pain the more of us that gather around you.

You can expect to have thousands of light beings in areas of your planet, where there is deep sadness and pain.

We congregate in these areas, we whisper, we chant, we sing, we dance, we do whatever it takes to expand our light and your light, to bring you out of sadness.

We also understand that you have requested some of these issues on your life path in order to grow. We will walk with you as a friend through the deepest and darkest parts of your path.

Think of us as if we are holding a light up, so you should see where your feet are going.

While we cannot take your pain away, we seek to offer friendship and companionship.

We are whispering about the next best possible actions that you can take, to bring yourself forward, to learn these lessons that you have chosen to learn more quickly so that you can again walk in the light

During these times of darkness in your life, it's like going on a train through a tunnel, it is necessary to go through the tunnel if we wish to get to the other side of the mountain.

Keep going. Our message today is, know that when you are going through your saddest, your darkest, your most painful times, we walk with you in the thousands.

We love you.

36. Grace is a quality that strives to enter your heart now

Within grace, there is hope and peace.

Think of a beautiful swan gliding on a still lake. Think about how beautiful it looks, feel the beauty in your own heart as you watch grace in your life.

The swan moves with ease, it's perfectly and completely in the now, doing what needs to be done, at this moment.

There is no need to think about tomorrow or next week or last week or last year. There is only to do what needs to be done at this moment now.

The swan is graceful, it does not think about being graceful, it just is graceful.

Imagine what it would be like if you allowed grace into your life and if you allowed effortlessness guide your steps every single moment.

Just by slowly bringing yourself into this moment today and every day these messages will bring grace back into your life.

Walk, talk and speak with grace today.

Find an image of a swan on a lake and hold it in your mind. We have said before the animals on this planet have much to teach you about finding God and the way to happiness.

You are graceful.

You have just allowed yourself to become otherwise, by interfering with God's plan for you.

Come back to us today.

You are a child of grace.

37. Gratitude without emotion is useless

We have spoken of gratitude before and today we'd like to bring your thoughts back to it. There is a belief that you need to be grateful for something, in order to bring more of that in.

While there is some truth in that, when you express gratitude for something in your life, in simple terms, the universe is pleased and wants to give you more. But this is also true for expressing anger, the universe is still pleased, as it reacts to your emotion and wants to give you more of the same.

The key behind getting more of what you really want is the EMOTION.

We have already told you that the words themselves that are expressed are not really that important.

Although some of you may react to certain words as they trigger emotions within you.

To get the most from gratitude, to use it to manifest what you really want, put emotion behind it.

Think about the emotion that you would most like to have. Is it fun, is it happy, is it sadness is it depression or is it joy? The choice is yours that is the absolute truth.

Although you may get yourself into a funk with one or more of these 'negative' emotions.

And you may need help, to literally pull yourself out of them.

After the awareness that we are sharing with you dawns on your mind, you realise that you have a choice to remain there. You have a choice how to feel and be in the world.

Gratitude without emotion is as useless and undirected as releasing a tissue into the wind.

Focus your gratitude work and give it all the positive emotion you can muster, and the universe will gladly respond to you and bring you more of the same.

This is a promise!

38. Peace in your toes

Are you curious?

Do you know how forgotten your toes are?

You are in every part of your body.

Yes in every part.

You inhabit this vehicle, although you don't always live consciously in every part of it.

You spend most of your time up in your head and occasionally in your heart when the emotion is strong enough.

And almost never in your toes!

Today do one simple thing, that will give you peace and a wonderful sense of grounding.

Wriggle your toes!

Remember what it feels like to place your toes in cool water, on the beach or imagine moving them in warm sand.

Bringing your attention and focus down into your feet and into your toes, will help you regain clarity and comfort and get you out of the worry zone in your head.

Doing this little exercise, using your imagination, adding how good this FEELS, will give you back your confidence and certainty.

Practice it today.

Wriggle your toes in the sand!

39. Avail of the mysteries the animal kingdom holds for you

There are many easy ways to relax and unwind.

None is more beneficial for you than to go outside and connect with the animal kingdom.

We cannot stress how important these beings are, for your spiritual and personal development.

We daily give praise and thanks to these gentle and wise beings, inhabiting the planet with you.

You will have a preference for the types of animals you are drawn to.

This preference is a clue, to the qualities you can use in your own life that these beings wish to impart.

For example are you a 'cat person'? Do you prefer dogs? Do you like tigers? What does listening to whale song do for you? What happens when you become interested in ants on your path as they carry weights and burdens much greater than seem possible for their tiny bodies?

What do you feel when an animal is tortured or hurt or in pain?

Some of you have numbed yourself to some extent and may even see these beings, as lower or of lesser importance than you. There is no blame here, it serves no purpose.

If you knew they were wise and had so much to teach you, you would sit up, take notice and listen.

Now you know.

It's that simple. Avail of the mysteries the animal kingdom holds for you.

One of their gifts is focus and relaxation and deep, deep peace.

We love you.

40. You are not who you think you are!

There is much more than the eye can see.

We can see you clearly.

We can also see the cloak of darkness that is this body of beliefs, ideas and patterns that you hold so close to yourself and live by each day.

You, as you think you are and most resonate with, is this being, who is a compilation of all those who have gone before you.

Your parents, your grandparents and many generations, have had effects on you and your mind that are interfering with your ability to see and feel and know God.

You are so much more. You must take our word for it today.

As you still have a while to go before this new seed begins to take root and grow inside of you. The potential we see makes us faint with joy.

You could literally command the heavens and the earth if you would only step into the truth of who you really are. We have hinted at it.

We have shown you glimpses in the hope that your true self will begin to stir, like a great giant that has slumbered for 1,000 years. Like sleeping beauty waking up and remembering who she is.

You are blinding light.

You are God's only child.

You are everything and everywhere.

You are me, and I am you.

Prepare to wake up to love.

For love is all there is, forever and ever.

41. You ask and we answer

When you make a request to God we rush to your side to help YOU fulfill this request.

Yes that is the missing ingredient.

YOU must actively create your reality as you would wish it to be.

All the requesting in the world will not change anything unless you take part.

When you ask for something and with enough emotion attached the universe will respond to you (with equal emotion). The universe will respond by allowing us to guide you to the next action that you must take to get you where you want to be.

The next action could be to relax, it does not always involve movement, and you do not need legs to manifest your greatest dreams in this world.

You only need to request the universe to meet you desires to change your world in some way, and the universe will respond to you with the next best step that YOU need to take.

Stop, breathe, think about what you want to happen in your life and see that vision in your mind. Now infuse it with as much positive emotion as you can muster then wait.

The next step may come as a hunch or a nudge, or an earth angel may step in to take your hand and bring you toward an opportunity.

YOU MUST TAKE ACTION TO CREATE THE LIFE YOU WANT!

42. We will send you earth angels

When you are not open to us, we will send you earth angels to help you on your path.

And when you *are* open to us, we will send you earth angels to help you on your path.

There will always be help available, the key as we mentioned before is in taking action.

God will always come to your aid; God will always watch over you, God sends us to you.

You send us to you.

The emotions you use during your life are a way of communicating with us.

We can see emotion as colour and flashes of light across the universe

We can literally see your distress, and we know instantly when you need us most.

Your emotion draws us to you; your action allows you to receive our guidance.

It's like picking up an invisible telephone that's ringing. Unless you pick up the phone and speak, the connection will not be made.

It is always up to you to pick up the phone, your emotion is like an SOS into the universe.

We immediately connect with you, we are with you instantly. Then it's up to you to start a conversation before you can hear us talking to you clearly.

Reading these notes is an action.

Meditation is an action.

Walking in nature is an action.

Sitting in your car for 5 minutes and breathing is an action.

You are in the command seat in your life.

43. Peace is your aim

Peace is your goal.

There are many options open to you.

You always have the choice.

We are always connected to you, helping you to find and regain peace in your life.

Bring the image of the swan to mind again.

It's so peaceful, as it glides across the water.

It's doing something though, its feet are moving beneath the water.

It takes action to have an effortless life and consistent action becomes a learnt behaviour and more action again each and every day after that becomes mastery.

With mastery comes peace.

Achieving mastery and peace is as easy as learning to drive a car or brush your teeth.

Both just take consistent action every day.

Even as little as 1 minute over a lifetime can accumulate, as a great store of peace that you can access when you need to.

44. Today just give us one minute

The phone is ringing.

We are calling you.

Take action, Pick up the phone!

Start the conversation.

We love you.

There is peace on earth.

45. 'Ain't no mountain high enough'

Every one of you would benefit from a spiritual practice.

How you carve out this practice and this time is up to you.

We have said as little as one minute a day for God will be enough to connect you to the divine, the invisible and to us your angels.

How many minutes you put in after that is up to you.

Like a new friendship, there might be some effort in the beginning; you will want to make time for that person in your life. You will call them regularly.

Relationships come and go throughout your life. But think of this as calling an old friend. Whenever you pick up the phone, it's like you were speaking yesterday, even if you haven't spoken for years.

That's the relationship we have.

We are old dear friends, we know each other intimately.

We had followed each other throughout our lives, dipping in and out, the relationship intensifying when it needed to, in order for us to receive the help we need in our lives.

We walk beside you today; we are always available to you.

We are awaiting your call and we will be there.

'Ain't no mountain high enough to keep us from you!'

46. Thy will be done

There is no way around this.

There is no other way to say it.

These words are all you need to understand how *you* create the life you are living.

If your will be done really and truly, then you can change anything you want, the relationship, the job, the health issue.

There are some places you think you have control and others were you completely relinquish your power.

It's like you've been brainwashed to believe you are less.

There is only sadness in living a life that's mediocre and that's less than you desire, love and deserve.

Claim it!

Ask for what you want.

Then claim it as yours.

Thy will be done.

Contemplate this today my love.

If this is true, what would you change in your life?

You've got the power we love you.

We love you.

47. Healing is possible

Healing is possible for all of you; there is no ailment that cannot be healed.

You are God, God is in you. We are the same.

You can heal your mind instantly, and then your body follows suit.

As you think about your body, so shall it be in the world.

When you focus on aches and pains, they will increase.

When you focus on health and vitality, this too shall increase.

When you feel weak, think strong, and your body will react to you, your thoughts and the words you use.

Add emotion for fuel.

There is little more to it.

This simple exercise should give you some insight into the power that's within you.

Claim whatever it is you want to happen!

I am strong!

I am healthy!

I am rich!

I am peaceful.

My mind is clear.

I have all the answers available to me that I need.

I am healed.

48. This place is filled with angels

Do you see those flashes of light, so fast that you can easily convince yourself, it was your imagination?

What if you could see these lights for longer periods and the colours deepened and became more intense?

You might begin to notice that you feel good when the lights are around.

You notice one or two colours more often.

You begin to recognise these lights as your angel friends, who are near you, clapping their hands with joy as you finally begin to really see how the world can be.

Right now this minute wherever you are, this place is filled with angels.

There are as many angels as grains of sand or blades of grass or stars in the sky.

We are infinite and more than you can see right now.

That amount of light would be uncomfortable for your physical eyes, but you can use your imagination.

Close your eyes right now and throughout your day, ask yourself; What would this space or situation look like if it were filled with angels?

How would it be different?

How would that feel?

49. Your light is love

There are many energy centres in your body and auric field.

Some are attached to physical organs.

Others are attached to your aura and related to either, how your soul once was physically on this planet or how your body and soul evolve and grow throughout many earth lifetimes.

Your soul seeks to grow constantly.

This growth is not defined to this lifetime you're living.

You have been here many times before.

You will return again and again, until infinity in different forms.

There is no completion. There is no ending. Your evolution will continue forever.

This is a creative universe, you are here only to grow and expand your light.

Your light is love. The density of your body can be released with love.

We share this with you today, to offer hope and comfort.

Your soul can never die; your soul is pure love.

Your body is just a great big overcoat that you wear while you are here this time.

In the pockets, are all your beliefs, generational and karmic ties, promises and vows.

But at any time you can choose to recognise that you are love.

The light of love has the power to blast through any material thing and change it.

50. We are everywhere you are

You don't need any special wisdom.

You don't need any particular time.

There is no way that we are not.

In your darkest moments and in your happiest moments, we are there always and forever.

You don't need any special spiritual practice.

You don't need any special combination of words or prayers, to bring us to your side.

You are worthy just as you are, in your life right now, at this moment in time.

We walk beside you, speak, and we can hear you.

Listen and you will hear us speak to you.

We are everywhere you are today.

We love you.

51. There is love on this earth now

Sometimes you think you need our help more.

It is in those moments that you will call out to us and in a moment of anguish your channels are clear, and you can clearly hear us communicate.

Your heart is open in the pain that you experience, like an open wound.

We are able to enter into your mind.

It is in your surrender of Will that we are able to enter into your mind and communicate with you clearly.

Saying something like this; 'God I give up, help me!' will open up your channels so you can hear us finally.

However, it doesn't have to just be in these moments of extreme anguish. You can choose at any moment to communicate with us.

You can choose at any moment to hear us clearly in your heart. Just let go of how you think that communication should be.

We do not always use words, written or spoken. Feelings, visions and sensations in your body are all ways that we use to communicate with you today.

You can use that phrase 'I give up God, I hand it over to you now, show me what I need to do!'

And God will send his angels to you instantly, to the place where your heart has opened.

There is love on this earth now.

52. All will be well

Happiness is just a thought away; there is no need to sacrifice a moment of your life in unhappiness.

Happiness is a sensation, a feeling, a knowing within you, that all will be well.

It's a simple message that you can train your mind to accept, with the constant repetition of this phrase today and every day.

'All will be well'

This can bring about so much peace and happiness. This phrase applied to any situation can bring happiness today. Whatever confronts you, whatever it looks like externally to you, say: 'All will be well, and so it is'.

You are loved.

53. Instead of expectations have acceptance

Your expectations are your downfall.

For when your expectations are not met, this can cause you anguish, and you doubt that we exist. You doubt that God can hear your requests. You doubt that God can help you in every way, in everything, in your life.

Stop expecting things to go your way, instead accept what is.

Accept that whatever is given to you today holds an essential lesson that will give you all the help you need in your life.

And until you learn the lesson this situation will continue.

Don't expect anything to change until you have learnt the lesson.

Instead give thanks today, whenever you are confronted with something beyond your understanding.

Instead, thank God for giving you this opportunity to learn something that is essential for your growth and your personal and spiritual development.

God never gives you more than you can handle.

You are complete.

Instead of expectations, bring acceptance to the situation and thank God for bringing you here.

Ask for our help to change the situation in the best possible way for you and everyone concerned.

Today release your expectations and just ask for love in this situation.

Have a grateful heart.

54. Everything is love

You are loved and you are light.

This is the truth.

No matter what is going on in your life at the moment on earth, the only truth that you need to hold in your heart is that you are loved.

Even closer to the truth, is that you are love and everyone, every being you come across today is also love.

No matter the situation, no matter the conflict, no matter what things look like.

Underneath everything, the truth is that you are all love.

Everything is love, there is nothing else.

55. I see love and light

What will you behold today?

What images will you allow to confront you on your day?

What part of your vision will you allow to shine more clearly?

You have two ways of looking at the world.

You can use your physical eyes and see the physical earth, this physical existence or you can choose to use your other sight and see the beauty and the light that is within everything on this planet.

This may be difficult to start with, as you have trained yourself to only use your two physical eyes.

First, you must accept that there is another way to see the life on this planet.

Just your acceptance and acknowledgement that there is another way to see, will open up your sight today and soon you will see it.

The love and the light are in everything, say to yourself today;

'I see with my true eyes, this world that I live in today. I see the love and the light within every being and everything'.

56. I release control to God

Where there is pain, there lives at the centre, a heart who has refused to see God in everything, who has refused to see that God is here within them and available for help all of the time.

Pain is as a result of control, wanting and trying to be in control of this life.

It is useless, time-consuming and tiring.

Let go of control today, hand it over to God, your creator, with a sigh of relief.

Hand over your burdens, hand over your sadness and hand over everything that you think is too heavy, too much for you to handle.

Give it to God, and we will gladly shoulder the burden with you or carry it for you.

If you are in pain today, emotional physical or mental pain, ask God to take it from you.

Say; 'I give this to you now God. I release control of the situation'.

And then rest and know that very soon a solution will present itself, to help you.

Today you are blessed.

57. We are all love

Each moment is a chance to welcome God into your life.

By God we mean, universal being, divine light, supreme bliss, great mystery..... insert whatever word you wish to use here. The closest description in your understanding is love.

Love is the essence which binds everything in this universe together.

More than that, love is the essence of everything that is on this planet, at this time and in this universe.

Everything that is, has been created from love and is love.

You have chosen to believe differently. You see yourself separate from God, you see yourself separate to us, your guardians, your friends.

You see yourself as a separate entity.

This is not true; love connects us all because love is everywhere.

We are all one, we are all love.

58. You are a clear channel for divine messages

There is a moment, this moment, right here, right now, that you can choose to connect to us.

This connection line is always open, from our side anyway.

You can choose to block the connection, with negative thoughts, destructive patterns of behaviour, and chemicals and food that are not good for your body.

Everything that you do affects this communication line.

Everything that you eat, everything that you say, affects whether the communication is clear or muddled.

You can start to change this today, by using your words and your mind and your conviction within you.

Use your wish for clarity, use your desire to connect with us clearly today and say;

'I am open to hearing my angel's voice. I am open to communicating with my angels; I am a clear channel for divine messages'

Say this over and over and over again. You can say it to yourself, tell the plants and whisper it to the traffic lights, the trees and the animals. You can say it out loud or inwardly.

'I am a clear channel for divine messages'

And so it is.

You are loved.

59. Rest!

Oh, we love it, when you rest, when you take a respite from the world, when you pull back and renew and rejuvenate yourself and your soul.

This is a perfect opportunity for us to speak to you.

When you are relaxed, you are open, you have released control.

You are in a state of rest, and you are open for us to offer healing to you at this time.

Your rest rejuvenates your body and your mind emotionally, spiritually and mentally.

On all levels, rest is so essential for your wellbeing, and it's also one of the easiest ways to communicate with us, even if it is for the most part, unconscious.

Your creator has given you this gift of sleep, has given you this gift of rest, where you release control, and you hand your body over to God for those few hours.

Later as you go deeper on this path with us and you deepen your experience of God and love, when you develop your own meditation practice, you will be able to use the same principles of sleep in your waking moments.

You will receive the same benefits of sleep, while in meditation.

You will use this time to consciously connect with God and love.

This will reduce the time you need to sleep and will rejuvenate you on a much deeper level than even sleep.

Rest often.

60. I give up control

These moments of distraction that you allow to take over your mind are a direct result of you trying to control things.

Again, please release the need to control your life, people, situations and experiences that you have every day.

We have spoken about this before, it's so important, we are reminding you now today.

Say to yourself;

'I give up control, I accept whatever happens to me today'.

Accepting doesn't mean that you have to understand it or even forgive. This will come later.

Today just accept my love.

There's a FREE Cutting the ties with your Guardian Angel Meditation to support you with this exercise **at:**

www.aishlingmooney.com/bookbonus

61. Peace is a state of mind

There are many ways to find peace.

There are many ways to bring peace to your mind.

For each of you, different ways will suit you and your particular experience on this planet at this time.

Some of you would prefer to walk in nature.

Some of you would prefer to move your body, dance, exercise or practice yoga techniques.

Some of you sit in meditation and some of you will take a nap.

All of these offer the opportunity to bring peace.

Even doing nothing sometimes can bring peace.

You say you want peace on earth.

Bring peace to your mind first. There is nothing to do.

Relax; it's not something you even need to think about.

Decide that you would like peace in your mind and in your heart today.

Ask us for help with this and know that it is already so.

62. Give up the struggle

Where were you when I needed you? Why don't you speak to me? Why can't I hear you now? You don't even exist!

This amuses us. We can feel your struggle, your fighting and your trying to take control of the situation.

We can feel your expectations. We can hear your demands for now, for more, like a child screaming for sweets before dinner.

We would ask you to stop the struggle. Just give it up. Stop trying to make things happen, the way you expect them to happen. Stop expecting God to behave in a certain way. Stop expecting your world or your life to be different. This struggle gives energy, to that which you do not want in your life.

Everything created requires energy.

Everything that you put your mind to, you give energy to.

You increase its potential to be created, to be a reality.

Stop the struggle. Think about what you do want to happen. Give that your thanks, give that your energy.

Give up trying to control and change what it is and bring your focus to how you wish to be.

Hold that image with conviction, with love and also with a knowing that *you* don't have to create this.

Give it up to God.

Manifestation is easy. It's your constant struggle and focus that makes it difficult.

Give up the struggle today my love.

Let us help you with that.

63. Go in peace

Peace on earth.

Peace in your own mind.

Peace in your heart.

Peace in everything you say.

Peace in everything you do.

Peace in solitude.

Peace and harmony.

Peace everywhere today for you.

Go in peace my sweet child and bring that peace everywhere you go today.

Let it shine in each footstep you take.

Walk in peace on this planet today.

64. Forgiveness is the key

The prophets came before us.

Many of you also walked this earth many lifetimes ago, reducing and vanquishing your karma.

There is only one reason you walk the earth today. That is to release karma.

To reduce karmic dues and to receive Karmic dues.

There's only one way to overcome the karmic cycle, and that is through love.

Forgiveness is the key to love.

Forgiveness will help you to release your karmic debt and to release others from future karmic debt.

Love is the only way to break the cycle, to increase your vibration and to accelerate your path of spiritual evolution.

Love is the way and the answer.

Forgiveness is the key.

65. Be ready to forgive

Imagine a triangle of love.

Close your eyes and see the triangle in your mind.

Place yourself in one corner and in the other corner, someone you love dearly.

Begin to fill this triangle with the emotion of love.

Feel the peace and happiness build within you, as this feeling of love just fills your own body and fills the triangle and fills the other person within the space.

In the final point of the triangle, place someone that you have difficulty forgiving.

Place this person in the triangle of love and even if it's difficult just allow this person to be filled with this love.

You don't have to understand this; you don't have to even know how this is possible. There is still part of your mind that resists this love for this person.

Say to this person; 'Even though I can't forgive you, I offer you the love in this space.'

You will never be ready to forgive; you will never want to forgive. But this is something that you must do for yourself. You must make a stand and start somewhere even if it's difficult.

The more difficult it is, the bigger the catalyst for change, the bigger the opportunity for huge transformation and growth in your own life.

As you forgive another, you give back to yourself.

For now, just accept this and be open to beginning this journey.

66. I love you, I forgive you

Bring back the triangle to your mind today.

This time, place yourself in all three corners and fill the triangle with love.

Bring back those parts, those feelings, those sensations of love that you felt for that person in your life that you love dearly. Now allow this love to completely infuse every single part of the triangle and your being. See the triangle in gold, see the light within the triangle of gold. See the love of golden light infusing the whole triangle and everything in it.

See the three parts of you in each point of the triangle.

Now bring those three parts together, in the centre of the triangle and say;

'I love you, I forgive you, I love you, I forgive you'.

Do this exercise at least 3 times today. It should only take a few minutes with effects that will reverberate right out into the universe and go right back through your family lines, to your ancestors and forward to all of your descendants.

I love you, I forgive you is all you need to say and do today to make a difference.

Love yourself as we love you.

67. I see love today

Focus on your third eye today.

That space on your forehead, between your two eyes.

Open your eyes today, say; 'Today I see love'.

This is so simple, but such a powerful exercise.

Try this throughout the day.

Whenever you have a moment, tap on your forehead say;

'I see love'

Click the link below to learn about Aishling's Forgiveness course to support you with this exercise.

www.aishlingmooney.com/bookbonus

68. Your desires are creating your reality

Where there is desire, there is potential for change.

Be very careful what you focus on now.

You, who have been reading these messages every day, are opening yourself up to us, to divine messages. You are becoming clearer, your energy uplifted, your sight is clearer, you begin to see with true eyes.

We have stressed how important this is to be careful with your desires.

Become mindful of what you are thinking about and what you are feeling.

Every feeling that you have is creating something in this universe.

Every feeling, every desire, that you have shoots out into the universe, like a rope or lasso attaching to whatever it is that you want.

If you continue to complain about your life while using all sights and senses, to think that which you do not want, that is the energy that you are sending out into the universe.

This is what you are calling more of into your life.

Use this power that you that you now have, to focus on what you really, really want.

These desires are creating your reality now. Own this, accept this and you will begin to really stand in your own power, and you will begin to truly create the life that you really want.

69. You must take the first step

What do you want?

Such a simple question, yet your mind flits around grasping on too many different things.

You say: 'I want this, I want that, I want those, I want these'.

And then you argue with yourself, 'but I can't have it, it's not possible. I don't believe it!'

This constant battle in your mind makes it difficult for you to really get what you want.

Most of the time you're focusing on what you don't want.

Then it's obvious that this is where you're giving most of your power and that this is then created in your life.

Every single one of you knows that Meditation would benefit you.

You all know that some spiritual practice will help you to still this vibrating mind.

You have read about the benefits, yet you still resist.

This is the part of you that wants to stay stuck. That wants to stay in this limbo of what you don't want. That wants you to stay separate from God and love, and the true reality.

You must be strong; you must make a stand for yourself and your mind. You must give yourself some consistent time, every single day, to be peaceful, to be quiet and to become a vessel for God's wisdom and love.

You must create that space in your life, even if it is as little as 2 or 3 minutes a day.

God will graciously accept whatever you can give, but you must take the first step towards God.

When you are ready, we are here, available to help you with this, just ask.

We love you.

70. Embrace the child today

Thank God for the children.

Thank you God for these beautiful beings, new, innocent and pure, who arrive here in a state of bliss and pure acceptance, loving everyone and every moment and herself completely.

They come and ask the universe to obey their will, they cry when they need food, comfort and love.

They expect their will to be heeded.

Actually, there is no expectation; there is just an is-ness and being in the moment.

Pure acceptance of self and life and what is.

You were once a child; you once lived in this state of being with ease without difficulty.

The child still dwells within you.

The child you no longer are, that child is screaming for your love and acceptance and protection.

Close your eyes right now and see yourself as a very small child.

Feel the love expand and grow in your own heart.

Feel that love enveloping the child, allow your heart to expand and just be filled with love for this child, for this part of you.

You deserve love; you don't have to be anything else, except yourself.

You are perfect, as you embrace that child today.

There is only love.

We love you.

71. Ask and ye shall receive

By now you start to feel the changes within you, happening as you read these messages every day.

You look forward to these words. They bring stillness within you, a certain amount of peace and calm.

They bring reassurance to your heart.

You begin to believe that you are not alone on this earth.

You begin to allow the possibility that angels exist and walk with you every day.

Angels are there to help you, in every single moment in your life and we have so much to teach you, so much to share with you.

All you need to do is be open to us, to accept that we exist and accept our help in your life.

Ask, and you shall receive.

This is a universal law that we are all bound by.

Ask and it shall be given unto you.

There are many ways to ask; through your words, your desires, your thoughts, but ultimately and most strongly through your feelings.

Focus on what you really want, feel how that would feel when it becomes a reality and we will do everything in our power to make it so.

We love you; we can never interfere with the divine will.

Ask, and you shall receive.

72. Peace is a step towards love

You are beautiful, you are serenity.

You are a peaceful garden.

When forgiveness reigns in your life again, there will be peace and absolute serenity, regardless of what's going on around you in the world and in your reality.

If you learn this vital lesson, this important too, life can never be the same again.

You will begin to continuously, each and every day, seek to forgive.

You seek forgiveness, in order to release and let go of accumulated karma.

You will always seek peace.

Peace is one of the steps towards love.

We love you today.

73. You are on the path to peace

Where there is hatred, sadness, doubt and fear, there is not God.

Although God is everywhere and love is the only reality in your existence, in your physical existence and vibration through all levels of the universe, *you* can choose at any moment to see the opposite.

It's free will, it is God's gift to you, but we can assure you, there is only love.

You *can* choose peace.

We know this is difficult for you to understand or even to believe.

Trust us, this will get easier.

As if you read these messages every day, you are opening your consciousness, and you are dismantling old beliefs and ideas about yourself and the world.

You are on the path to peace.

Things are changing, even if you can't see that right now.

But soon you will look back, like seeing an old photo of yourself and see the beauty within you and wonder why you didn't see that beauty at that time.

Someday you will look back at this moment and wonder why you couldn't see.

Please trust us, there is only love.

74. Our commitment to you is everlasting

When will you agree with us?

When will you choose to see a peaceful life for yourself?

When will you choose to trust our truth?

Always, when you have had enough of this reality, when it just becomes too painful for you not to see love. Then you will come to us, you will search for us again, and the beauty and the wonder of this is that we have never left you.

No matter what you do, what you say, where you are or what you believe, we cannot leave your side.

Like a betrothal, our commitment to you is everlasting.

We have promised the almighty, that we will care and protect and guide you every single step of your life.

We cannot break that vow.

When you are ready, we are here with you.

We truly love you.

75. How will you direct your love today?

You are me and I am you.

The separation that we see and feel is not true.

You are connected and we are connected with everything else in this universe.

The animals, the trees, the plants, the flowers, the air that we breathe and the dust particles of life in our atmosphere.

There is one thing that ties all of this together, and that is love.

That is the energy and the glue that holds this universe together.

Without this glue of love, your reality would crumble.

It just wouldn't exist.

This love that you are made of gives you limitless power, to form and transform your reality.

You think the power is determination.

You think its focus.

You think you manifest, by your desires and the emotion that your place in those desires.

The full truth is...because you are made of love, and this is the most powerful substance in the universe, (in fact it's the only thing that exists) this is how and why you can create whatever you want.

Whether you perceive what you create, as good or bad is up to you

You have been given this power.

You must choose to learn how to use it.

How will you direct your love today?

76. We are in the quiet places

Where are you today?

What river or rushing ocean have your thoughts taken you on?

You are like a boat in a storm, moving this way and that way, almost toppling and tumbling over into disaster, trying to steady yourself and create stability on a moving ocean, a rocking boat.

It's almost impossible, my love.

But if you will just go with the rocking, go with the flow of the movement that's around you on this earth today...

Just go with the flow of your life, move with the waves, sway your hips and allow the rhythm to guide you forward.......

How do you hear this music, this rhythm?

You must quiet your mind.

Stop, pause, breathe, reflect.

A few moments of peace and contemplation each day would be enough to calm the biggest storm in your life, because in that peace we are there for you.

77. We have the map, let us show you the way

You think you have no time.

You think there is never enough, but everyone has the same amount of time in a day.

When you signed your sacred contract, you knew what you needed, to accomplish it.

You knew how many minutes and hours and months and years you would need to complete this task.

God agreed to all of your demands.

You have everything you need to complete your mission within you and around you in this world.

You *are* on your path.

You are completing your life purpose right now.

Today everything that's happening is something that you need to learn.

It's another part of the puzzle, of who you are meant to be during this lifetime on Earth.

You are in charge, we are your guide, and we can see your full contract.

We have the map.

Anytime you feel lost, come find us, and we will show you where to go next.

You are deeply loved.

78. Go to your heart space

Think of your heart as a comfortable sitting room, with nice big cosy armchairs, chaise lounges and snuggly sofas.

Go there now, to those plush surroundings, beautiful textures, pillows and rich colours.

Nourish your soul.

Go there now.

Fall into the comfort, the comfortable place of your own heart.

Lie down on the cushions, sink into the sofa.

Breathe in the beautiful smells of incense and fresh flowers.

Enjoy the rich colour's that surround you and nourish your soul.

Notice the colours and notice one in particular that seems to be more vibrant than the others.

Take a beautiful, comfortable blanket in this colour and wrap it around your body now.

As you lay down, relax, breathe, heal.

This colour is healing for you right now in your life.

Notice your angel sitting on another chair nearby.

Ask them any questions about anything in your life at the moment. Maybe an issue or situation that may be bothering you, that's causing you some conflict.

Talk to your angel now in your heart space.

Explain the issue and ask for help.

And so it is.

Go about your day today, and you remember the nourishment and healing that you received in your heart,. You will find a resolution for your problem through an overheard conversation or in a miraculous healing, maybe in a surprise phone call, or a random thought.

Somewhere today, you will see the solution.

Relax and breathe and remember your heart space as you walk on the earth today.

To access your FREE Guardian Angel Meditation and other bonus meditations to support you with this exercise go to:

www.aishlingmooney.com/bookbonus

79. Trust your own sense of appreciation

Colours are an important part of your world.

You can see us show ourselves in colour.

Different coloured orbs and lights represent different vibrations and energy that we use to reveal ourselves to you.

What colours have you begun to notice around you more each day?

What colours are you drawn to?

What clothes do you wear most often?

For each chakra point, in your body, there is a matching colour. By bringing that colour into your life, you bring healing to these chakra points. You also bring healing to every single issue, that's related to that point.

You don't even really have to know what you are doing.

Just follow your own sense of appreciation.

The colours you love and like and desire are the ones that you need for your journey.

Each colour has it on healing vibration within it.

Trust your bliss, trust what gives you pleasure and that will also give you healing.

80 A little knowledge of colour

You can use a little knowledge of colour to help you on your path.

Green brings peace.

Pink is love.

Red is passion.

Yellow is wonderful creative mind.

Blue is pure expression.

Indigo is insight and wisdom.

White is spirit and clarity.

Gold serene divine communication.

Black is grounding and protective.

Orange is happy and sociable.

Magenta is divine Goddess, powerful Goddess.

Turquoise is health and happiness and connecting with innocent love.

Play with colour in your life, allow it to guide you.

As we have said before, follow your bliss with this process. Learn through awareness of pleasure, what colours attract you. These will bring healing to your heart, your body and mind.

We send you silver angels to lift you up and fine tune your aura, so you will receive clear messages from us every day.

81. We are in your belly

We are in your belly, we are relaxed and at peace here, even if it feels uncomfortable for you.

There is no part of your body that is not beautiful.

This is an untrue observation that you make based on ideas and perceptions that you have collected over lifetimes *and* from decisions you have made yourself and from decisions others have made for you.

You have chosen to believe these decisions and beliefs.

There is no place, we are not.

All of you is beautiful, all of you is divine, all of you is love.

Please make a choice today my love to allow us to help you, to release these beliefs.

They really don't help or serve you in any way anymore. Everything has its purpose, every choice you made, has brought you to now. They have all been correct and according to what you needed to learn.

Nothing is graded as good or bad, it's all just a necessary part of your growth and development.

If you could see yourself as we do, without attachment to what is happening on the physical plane.

If you could see yourself as a being of light, having just one experience of many on this planet at this time.

You have been here before, you will come again.

This perspective today will help you to see the awesome nature of your true light body.

You are perfect exactly as you are and we love you more and more each day.

82. Love is my religion

What is religion?

A collection of beliefs based on a story, cycles and leaders, hierarchies and different steps to God, whatever name is placed upon her. Great Mystery, Yahweh, Allah, Divine Light, The Universe, Universal Energy...

All religions are searching for the same thing.

Devote yourself to love; attempt to find God in your own heart.

Allow religions to guide you some of the ways, but always come back to your own heart. We are there with you. You will find your sacred contract here. We can remind you of your mission.

Use religion to help you make sense of the healing and guidance behind the words, but ignore the doctrine and anything that is condemning or dictating or that makes you feel shameful.

Focus on love.

Go to your own heart for a short time every day, and you will know with certainty that this is the place that you need right now.

The first step is going to your own heart.

This is the first step to find the truth.

83. We are waiting for you

How long does it take to get to my heart? You asked.

About as long as it takes you to read that last sentence.

Go there now and now and now.

It's instant, it's a thought away.

Go there now.

We are there waiting for you.

84. Just one minute

Imagine if you were to go to your heart for one minute, every waking hour and then the habit would continue while you slept.

Imagine in 12 hours, you would have 12 minutes with us each day.

You might say 12 minutes is so little.

1 minute is more than none.

1 second is more than no time at all.

Transformation is instantaneous. There is no gap.

There is no need for endless hours of devotion in order to find God.

To find us, just 1 minute will make the difference.

1 minute each hour will make even more of a difference.

Think of this minute, like recharging your battery and plugging in your electronic device, so that you can continue to use it.

If you don't recharge, it dies.

If you don't recharge your soul, it forgets itself, it allows chaotic ego to take charge again

1 minute in your heart every hour or as much as possible each day, recharge your soul, your spirit and your mind.

This steady's you and gives you confidence.

Go there now, we are waiting.

85. Give yourself time

You may be convinced that you don't have time for us.

You may be sure there isn't enough time for you.

The difference is that you choose where to spend your time.

Everyone gets the same amount of time every day.

How will you spend your day today?

How much time will you take for your soul and for yourself?

No one else will give you this time my dear, no one else has it to give.

Your time is yours; how you spend it is up to you.

Please give some back to you.

86. You are blinding light

There is a light inside you that is blinding.

If you could see what we see, you would be in awe.

This light has been hidden from you, by yourself.

Your ego who was your protector, has become your enemy.

Your ego hides what cannot be hidden.

Only through illusions and mirrors.

There is a light inside you, and sooner or later it will be revealed.

You can choose right now today, to start to reveal that light, one tiny chink at a time.

Brick by brick dismantle the walls of your illusion and pain.

Then like the walls of Jericho, allow your belief in yourself and God to bring these walls crashing down.

Blinding light throughout this earth

Never night again.

87. Solitude is not an option

Solitude looks like an option.

You think you have a choice.

Yes you can choose not to do it, but if you want to achieve peace in your life then there really is no choice, but to embrace solitude.

The answer to peace lives deep in your own heart and to access that place, you must go quiet and you must learn ways to quiet your mind.

You must stop the chitter-chatter of your mind.

Solitude is not an option.

It is an essential practice that you must devote some of your time to, every single day.

Start to see it as an essential part in your journey of self-discovery every day.

88. Learn to control your feelings

To change the way you feel you must feel differently.

This sounds like a contradiction and may even cause you irritation, as you consider this simple message.

You have control over your feelings, or they can control you at any moment.

They probably control you most of the time, but you have a choice to learn a new skill today and learn to explore and understand your feelings.

When you can control your feelings, you can control your thoughts.

It's just another way to achieve the same thing, which is peace and love in your own heart today and every day.

89. Match your feelings to the change you want to achieve.

You all want to change; to change your job, your relationships, your hair and your life.

Some of these changes seem small and insignificant.

Some of them seem large and impossible.

Our question is; *how are you feeling about all of this today?*

The ability to change anything in your life is related to how you feel about it right now.

If you want to change your hair and your thoughts are saying you don't have money to pay for a hairdresser, you begin to feel irritated, angry and even sorry for yourself. This is absolutely the complete opposite to how you would feel if you change your hairstyle.

Really think about this now.

If you change your hair and it helps you to feel you feel happy, sexy, satisfied, younger, that is your end result. That is how you should feel about the change you are about to make, and that will create the change in a much more effortless way than anything else you can do.

You say you want to change. Think about this carefully today; what do you want to change? And most importantly; how do you feel about that?

Is there a match or mismatch?

90. Saturate your thoughts and ideas with love

The fastest way for you to change anything in your life, especially when you cannot control your feelings is to feel love.

Feel love, see love and saturate your thoughts and ideas with love. Think about someone or something that you love dearly and carry that feeling through to everything else that you want to change in your life.

So you want to move house, yet the move fills you with anxiety and worry and fear although you believe that it's the best thing for you right now.

Think about someone you love. Allow feelings of love to arise within you and your heart. Fill your body and your mind with this love, with this memory of gratitude and peace. Allow an absolute overflowing love and gratitude to fill your thoughts and now bring to your mind the thing you want to change.

Think about the move you would like to make and now feel the feelings of love and gratitude, do this daily, even for a few minutes, and you can achieve miracles in your life.

Love is the only balm that heals all thoughts and processes that the ego has hijacked.

Listen to love.

Feel love in your heart now and apply that to everything in your life.

Achieve miracles.

91. It takes courage to listen to your heart

How many of you say yes, when you mean no?

How many of you move forward, when you really need to pull back?

How many of you give more than you need to give, emotionally, mentally and physically?

How many of you stop and pause before making your decisions? Especially those decisions about where your energy must go.

Make it a daily practice now.

In the morning, invite your angels and God into your life and ask for help in each decision that you need to make today.

Make it a practice to pause, stop and take a breath, even if only for a moment.

Go into your heart and ask yourself; *what do I really, really want?*

It will take courage at first to even listen to yourself and then more courage to take steps according to your heart.

When this is practiced sincerely and honestly, it will do much to restore your energy back to you.

We love you.

You're doing so well.

92. Practice makes perfect

It's called a spiritual practice because that's what it takes, practice.

Or consistent effort each and every day.

It can be as little as one minute or as much as one hour at selected times, throughout your whole day.

Whatever practice you decide to do, you must commit to it and then follow through.

Think about learning to drive a car or any new skill; first, you must decide you want to do it, then you must decide how and what would be involved in helping you achieve your goal.

You must decide the steps, and you must allocate time from your life to achieve them because everything takes time.

The same is true for a spiritual practice. Having a daily spiritual practice will help you to learn to remember love and forgiveness.

These concepts are new to you.

You cannot expect to get them straight away.

Neither would you expect yourself to know how to drive a car after one lesson.

Today just open yourself up to the possibility of having a spiritual practice, that brings you back to your own heart.

We love you.

Keep going.

You are amazing.

93. All Masters were once Novices

Being Spiritual it's not just for now and then.

It's not something that you do on weekends or when you have time.

It's not something that optional, in your life.

Being Spiritual needs to become part of your BEING.

Be with yourself every day.

It is a spiritual practice, and it does take practice.

It takes quality time each and every day in your heart space.

In the beginning, it feels like a trial and it's an effort, but with time it is easier to do, like brushing your teeth or driving your car.

After a lot of practice comes expertise and then with more practice the expert becomes a master.

It becomes effortless.

The effortlessness means mastery.

All masters were once novices.

All masters had to begin somewhere.

Just start today where you are.

You are loved.

94. Colours are nourishing for your soul

Your world is colourful, including the plants, the trees and the people that you see.

There is colour everywhere in your life and in your world.

This is not a coincidence.

This is not a mistake.

You need to see this colour and feel this colour in your environment.

It is a healing medicine for you.

These colours are nourishing for your soul.

As you go about your life every day, notice the different seasons, in different colours and shapes and shades that surround you and your environment.

How does it affect you?

Blue skies, beautiful flowers, roses in bloom and a sea of dandelions or a big old oak tree ancient and wise.

Everything in your environment has it a place and purpose in your life and the colours speak to your soul, in a way your mind and logic can never understand.

Go outside and love the trees, love the grass and all of it, as we love you.

95. Symbols are signposts

Take the symbols from the plant and animal kingdom that you already use to nurture yourself.

Think about your favourite animal or your favourite flower and create a symbol of that being and place it somewhere you can see it every day.

You can infuse it with this new meaning, and this symbol will help you to achieve your highest potential.

The symbol can be a butterfly or a particular colour that resonates with you.

The easiest thing is to just think of those things that you love.

Love is the sign post that you are going in the right direction.

You will start to see references to this symbol everywhere in your life.

It will become a starting point, a middle point and an endpoint for you.

When you are at a crossroads, you will find the symbol in front of you in overheard conversation.

We will use the symbol that you have infused with purpose, to communicate with you.

The symbols are your sign posts that angels exist and walk with you every day.

We are guiding your every step, and we will use whatever symbols you give us to communicate with you.

The symbols on their own have no power, it is the meaning and significance you give them that creates the energy behind them to manifest whatever you want in your life.

Play with this for a while and see what happens.

96. There is a reason for everything

We know it is difficult to understand or sometimes even accept.

It is your perception that your life is wrong that causes you to feel even more pain.

Your life is exactly as you asked for it to be.

Before you arrived on this physical planet, you sat with us, and we discussed what you wanted to learn and achieve, while you were here this time.

You decided to do it all.

Sometimes we advised you against the hardest choices; it is always you who asks for the hard assignments.

We just offer graciously to be there to guide you, when you forget about God and the power you have in your own heart.

God never gives you more than you can handle.

You have chosen it all.

Just pause for a moment and ask yourself;

What if I chose all this? Then what does it really mean?

What could I possibly learn from this situation?

And there lie the jewels and the power.

Asking this question puts you back in the command seat in your life.

Go ahead, try it, keep an open mind.

We love you.

97. The reason you are here is to find love

If there is one ultimate reason for you to be alive and experiencing this life, it is to find love.

The search looks like an external one, as you roam about your life on a physical quest in search of love and a release from pain.

However, it is actually an internal one.

You will fight against it because it is easier to look without than within.

Read that last statement again.

When you focus on what is lacking in your life and what you are without, and that you have no control over, it can make you feel powerless.

When you focus on what you have achieved, on what you have learned and how well you're doing, love begins to blossom in your heart again.

As that flower unfolds and blossoms inside you, open up and love begins to flow outward into your world again.

The only reason you are here is to experience this love that is within you, right now today.

It's easy to find. The key is gratitude, for where you are, regardless of how it all looks externally.

This exercise takes time and some daily practice, but you can do it. It's nourishment for your soul and will help you smile a bit more every day.

We love to see you smile.

It is our privilege to support you on this journey.

98. It was always about love

You have been studying this programme for a little while now, you have received our teachings and our words.

You have felt them in your heart.

We have spoken of many things.

Can you see that the most important message that we can share with you is about love?

No matter what trials you face in your life, if you can find some love somewhere in your heart, this will sustain you through the challenging times.

Love is the boat and the captain and the compass.

If you have love, you will survive.

Start today with just this tiny morsel and whatever challenge you are facing, find something you love about yourself or your life and focus on that.

Fan the flames of it to make it grow.

In the beginning it may be weak, with practice it can get stronger.

Remember we are with you on the boat and everywhere.

You are never truly alone.

An angel walks beside you today and every day.

We love you.

99. You are on purpose

The phrase 'life purpose' can be deceiving and can take you off track.

You are *always* on purpose. You are *always* on the right track.

You are *always* walking towards love and God.

You are *always* returning to God and to your real home.

Every outward step you take on this physical path in your life, brings you one step closer to God.

No one has a better or worse path and no one goes astray.

We never leave you.

We have vowed to walk with you, and we will go where you go.

We are not afraid of the dark because we know it is an illusion.

We know there is only light and there is only love.

You are walking towards love.

It doesn't matter if you choose to walk through a dark tunnel or in the light. We are there.

We are guiding you and you are always walking towards God and love.

There is no other way.

There is nothing else to do.

100. You are the milestone

'Milestone: a significant stage or event in the development of something.'

Oxford dictionary online

Can you feel it within you, how important his moment is in your life right now?

You are standing on sacred ground.

When you walk, it is on sacred ground, with sacred feet.

You are on a sacred mission, and you haven't realised it until now.

Whatever has happened to bring you here has been a necessary part of your journey.

We have walked beside you; never for one single moment have we left your side.

And we have reminded you of your beauty, that you are love and loved by God.

Even in your darkest moments, we could see your light shining through.

The journey is only really beginning now my friend.

You have learned what you needed to take you here and you are ready for the next leg of the sacred path.

Rest here awhile and celebrate today in whatever you can and want.

Dance, sing, love, chant, be and do whatever brings you joy.

Today is a special day, and your achievement is being heralded by angels everywhere.

Can you hear us singing your name?

We love you.

Note from Aishling

If you're like me, then you may be tempted to just keep going and not take your angels advice and pause today, to celebrate how far you've come on this journey.

I get it, you like to work and there's always more to do. You don't have to take the full day off! (Unless you want to) Just mark out some time in your calendar today to pause and reflect and celebrate your success. If you look at your calendar and see it's full, ask yourself 'what could I move to another day?'.

When I've resisted taking time to relax, review and celebrate, strange things happen like my computer stops working or a client cancels or my kids get sick and I have to take time off to BE with them.

Once when I had pushed myself too hard without any time off and was set to continue, the universe had other ideas. I experienced panic attacks and anxiety and had to take six weeks completely off work. *(You can read the whole story on my blog www.aishlingmooney.com/breakthrough1)*

Each time I thought I was feeling well enough to go back to work something happened, my computer got a virus, then it completely died, my phone got stolen, one of my social media accounts was totally unpublished and I couldn't reach my community and share my services anymore.

The moral of the story is that if you don't make time (and in angel terms it takes really very little 1 to 3 minutes) the angels may 'help' you make the time.

My advice is to create some space for yourself to just pause today and celebrate. It really is that important. Plus you get to celebrate with the people that you love as well, if you want to. You can decide to celebrate alone or with those you love.

Much love

Aishling xxx

Today would be a good day to make time to access your free Angel book bonuses to support you, including; your FREE Guardian Angel Meditation. Go to:

www.aishlingmooney.com/bookbonus

101. The beginning of something, is also the end of something

For every step forward you take in your life, you leave something behind.

You are always shedding your past.

You cannot take any of it with you in any physical way.

Think about the clothes you wore as a child, where are they now?

They are memories in your mind.

Think about your childhood, it is only memories that seem to bring it into reality.

The truth is that none of it was ever real or lasting.

The only place where all of life as you see it, is in your memory.

In later life sometimes even this betrays you.

Your memory can be a lie.

Think about that for a moment.

Can you really be sure that it all actually happened?

Ok, stop the games and scrambling around in your mind. 'But, But, But...'

It doesn't serve you today or us.

This question was just to get you thinking about what is real and what is not.

102. All the world's a stage

Your mind up till now has had control over you.

You gave it this control.

We are here today to ask you to become aware of this.

Just this awareness will be the journey back to you taking control again.

It is easier for you to give over control, to your mind and your ego.

It can seem very sure of itself and knows exactly what to say to you, to make you believe in it.

It is quick to scold and blame and shame you in every area.

We are here to remind you of your beauty today, and that essence within you that cannot be tainted or changed in any way, by anything that has ever happened to you.

Imagine an actor on a cinema screen, acting out his part in the show.

When the show is over, she goes back to being herself; she is only playing a part for a while.

That's what living on earth is like for you.

Shakespeare said 'All the world's a stage'

You can choose how to act and react in your life, we will teach you how.

103. Through Angel's Eyes

These lessons are deeper, yes that's true.

They have a slightly different energy.

You have signed up for this series of messages, and even though you may not have read every single one, they are working on your mind, to help you to change and see the world in different and more positive ways.

Actually, through this series of messages, you will learn to see you and your world, as we see it all.

You will learn to see through angel's eyes, of pure love and compassion for yourself and everything that your life journey has brought to you, to experience and to live so far.

We see a shining light, as we look at you.

We see love, as your true essence.

We see this world as a bright star in the galaxy, offering hope and dreams fulfilled, for many souls who wish to work through karma and evolve as high as they can, on the path to ascension.

You are pure and true love.

There is nothing else to know.

You are loved so deeply, my sweet and dear child.

Look through our eyes and see your beauty.

Feel our love for you today.

104. We agreed to walk with you through it all

Today we ask your unconscious mind a question; ***what do you want to achieve in this lifetime?***

It doesn't matter if you don't fully understand this question or even know the answer.

Just by allowing us to ask your unconscious mind will remind you that this question has already been asked and answered.

Before you were born, we sat with you in a sacred space and you were asked this question.

You reflected on your past, and all that had happened to you as a soul, from the very first spark of your existence and you knew intuitively, what the next step was.

We agreed to walk with you through it all, the joyous times and the difficult times.

We know everything about you, all you are, have been and seek to become.

And whether you can acknowledge this or not, you are exactly on track in your life.

No matter what is going on, it's part of your sacred contract, and it will all make sense when it's your time to leave and return to spirit again.

This question will affect your dreams and thoughts in the days ahead.

You don't need to do anything, just be aware as your memory returns to you.

You are doing so well.

We're enjoying the journey.

105. You are God's light

There is nowhere we cannot be.

There is no place in your mind, your body, your soul or this physical and spiritual existence that we cannot be.

God gave us the task to accompany you on this journey and that means in every aspect, including your imagination.

We are recording all of it, in order to help you to grow and understand yourself more deeply.

Think of yourself on a quest, you have left your home with God to venture out into the world and experience all that it has to offer, in terms of physical, emotional and mental experiences.

Sooner or later the Voyager always returns to God.

We are your guides and your servants.

Ask us to help you, and we cannot deny you.

It is our sacred contract to remind you of yours and to show you the way, when you feel lost or out of control.

It's all an illusion of course; your soul is always in control.

Your ego just thinks it's the boss, but we know differently, and we can help you remember who you really are.

You are God's light, journeying this physical plane, having many adventures and experiences and creating stories to tell at the campfire, when you return home.

We can't wait to hear all about it, all over again.

You bring us so much joy.

106. Every second of the journey is rich with wisdom and beauty

Be grateful for every second of the journey.

Every second has a lesson that you need to learn.

Whether that's appreciation of a beautiful flower or compassion and forgiveness for someone who you believe has hurt you.

Every second of the journey is rich with wisdom and beauty, and by appreciating it all no matter what, you will grow and learn in leaps and bounds.

Your ego would have you moan and complain about everything that you think is wrong with you and your life.

Your ego hopes to keep you stuck so you will not complete your journey.

It fills you with fear and worries and doubts, about all that lies in front of you and the pain you feel when it does something that you don't understand or agree with.

Your ego also encourages you to hurt another with your words and thoughts and deeds.

Try appreciating just one thing every single day about this journey and your life. This will give you back control of it all.

You will put yourself back in the driver's seat and then we can sit with you and show you where you need to go next.

But you will drive the car, you will take control of your life, and you will carry out words, thoughts and deeds that bring you joy and love and increase the light we can see within you.

Today, sit and say 'I'm grateful for all of it' and begin to list everything about your life, the good, the bad and the ugly and give thanks and praise to God, for every second you have lived so far.

When you give thanks, the heavens fill with a chorus of angels taking this sound and vibration and magnifying it throughout the universe, to enhance life everywhere.

A simple word or thought or deed of thanks, multiplies many times and positively affects the universe you live in and beyond.

107. Speak kindly to yourself

Speak kindly about yourself and your body and your past.

Speak as you think a graceful, elegant and compassionate person would speak about you.

Speak as if you are the Dalai Lama or another spiritual leader or living saint and use your imagination to see and hear them speak kindly about you and all that you have accomplished while you've been alive, this time on earth.

You can disassociate if you wish at first and imagine that praise and love descending on someone else's ears and mind, body and soul, someone you may believe deserves it more.

Try this now;

Choose someone you admire and know as a 'Good' person..

Now see someone whose work you respect. See them; treat this person with the utmost kindness and respect. See them shower adoration and compassion and understanding on this person. See that person glowing and growing and becoming lighter and softer, under this shower of love and goodwill.

Now take that person out of the picture and put an image of you in there instead. Watch as you receive all of that love, just for you.

Now take one more step and find yourself in your own body, looking through your own eyes and receive this love for yourself completely. Absorb it and allow it to fill you up inside and out, pure understanding and love, like a warm blanket of protection.

You are truly loved, my sweet child.

If you just could accept this today, nothing would ever harm you or take your mind from God and love again.

108. A simple flower, your greatest teacher

You know there are levels of beauty and ecstasy that you could reach with your own mind if you wished.

Take a simple flower, as one of your greatest teachers and this little exercise alone could show you the love you really are.

By appreciating something outside, you allow love to blossom in your own heart.

Take your favourite flower (preferably in a tranquil outdoor setting), although if you can't do this right now, just find somewhere peaceful where you won't be disturbed.

Begin to examine the flower. You are looking for beauty and symmetry.

Turn it over in your hands and examine every part of it, treat it like a sacred object that's worth a lot of money. It's been taken from a sacred place and given to you to enjoy. You realise it's priceless and sacred and you hold it with awe and adoration.

See it with your eyes at first and then feel it within your heart. As you look at the flower and become entranced with whatever part of it lifts you and your energy, you increase the love within your own body, mind and soul.

You cannot appreciate and love anything on this planet without sending some love into your own heart. As you love something externally, you will feel it in your heart. Try it right now. It may be a subtle sensation at first, which will get stronger each time you try this.

Imagine what would happen to you, if you walked in a beautiful forest and admired and loved every single plant and flower that God had placed in your path. Imagine the love that would fill you up.

This is a spiritual practice that will help you love yourself, by loving something outside of you.

Enjoy it as soon as possible.

109. Just say YES!

Think about the trees and remember that they take in, whatever you expel that's toxic and make it safe again for you to breathe.

How much does the tree love you, to do this for you?

Large fish travel long distances across the oceans and make a point of stopping at certain places. The smaller fish living there eat all of the debris and sickness, from the bigger fishes back and body.

How much do these little fish, love the bigger fish, to do this for them?

There are people on your planet, who go out of their own way to offer kind words, deeds and thoughts to others.

How much do these people, love others to do this for them?

The truth is, no being does it for another, it does it because it is good for themselves.

The trees require the toxic substances to grow and evolve themselves, the small fish feed and fill themselves on whatever would cause the other fish sickness, and people who offer kindness do so because it makes them feel good within their own hearts.

This might sound a bit strange but think about this; if you were motivated to do whatever makes you feel good and if you were motivated to do whatever filled your heart with gratitude and kindness and this made you feel good, wouldn't this be a good thing?

The world works in beautiful symmetry, God has made it so easy for you do what's good for you.

It will feel good to do it, and you'll want to do it more often. Life is actually quite effortless, and you will always know what to do if you follow God's path.

Your ego will try to take control and tell you otherwise, that you need to plan and struggle and make things complicated and difficult, to get where you want to be.

We already know where you want to be, you told us so in your sacred contract, before you came here.

We hold the map, your ego does not.

Your ego would have you lost in a maze of fear and doubt and worry and stress.

Let us take your hand today, let us show you the way of ease and love.

Just say yes, and that's the first step to allowing the illusion to crumble and fall away revealing the true light of you.

Just say YES!

Today would be a good day to access your free angel bonuses to support you with this book and these this exercises at:

www.aishlingmooney.com/bookbonus

110. Rest for renewal and regeneration

Regular breaks are essential.

Even God rested on the seventh day, according to the Bible story.

There are two important elements to this sentence that God created and he rested, and he did it on the seventh day.

It is important to rest regularly, and it is important to rest as part of your sacred ritual of renewal and regeneration. Every one of the holy books tells of moments, where great prophets, kings and men rested before any great task or before a battle or even before death.

There is a pause before the next phase of existence. However that will look. Did you know that every seven years the human body has completely renewed itself; it has shed every single physical cell and has new ones that were not there before.

Did you know that rest is an absolutely essential part of this physical emotional and mental process called life on earth?

You know now.

Without proper rest, you cannot renew fully. Or you interfere with the process in some way.

There is, of course, a time when you will need less sleep and more sleep, depending on what's going on in your life, what battles you have to face tomorrow or what tasks you have agreed are part of your path.

But think of sleep and rest as a battery of energy that will serve you in your life. You can use meditation and your spiritual practice as well, to give you the resting space you need.

You must look at periods of rest as essential to your spiritual, physical and emotional development.

Your ego will try to tell you otherwise as usual.

Your ego will try to tell you that you need alarm clocks and do without proper rest and respite, it will tell you to keep going, to keep moving, striving, and struggling to make your life happen.

We tell you to relax and to rest, that this will give you more than you need in times of stress than anything else you could physically do.

You will have to trust us with this information as it may seem contrary at the moment in your life.

We can feel the 'buts' in the air.

Our lessons will get clearer the more you journey on this path.

111. Bliss inside

There is bliss inside of you; it takes up no space at all. It's like a whisper of emotion that starts in your belly and travels throughout your body depending on what's going on in your life and how you want to express it.

Even when you are angry there is still bliss in your body somewhere.

It is the life force that rushes through your veins with every heartbeat.

It is enhanced and brought forth in moments of happiness and intense clarity in your life.

It is quiet, and it is also still.

It is always there inside of you.

To find it you need just stop what you are doing for a moment and seek it out.

Stop and bring your attention to your breath and think; If I wasn't in control, who would be?

Ask it again and again. This question asked in silence and aloud with a sincere questioning heart has the power to shake your vibration to the core. It has the power to release you from your ego who has hijacked your system.

It's time my love, to take your life back.

It's time to live from this beautiful and natural place of bliss and sacredness.

It's time.

We love you, you are doing so well.

Well that's it for now.

112. Find your soul, and you will find peace.

That you have to strive for peace is an illusion.

Peace is already inside of you now.

We know these statements can cause you pain, even as you come to terms with them. You want to shout and scream at us, that we know nothing of your life on earth and all the struggles you need to face every day.

We are absolutely aware of what is actually going on, and we are aware of everything else as well. We have wings which give us this amazing perspective. We can go as high as we wish and see the situation from all angles.

We can also see it from within your own heart and mind. We can see your inner circuitry and your auric field. We can see way back into your past and a million years into your future.

We can see it all, and we are here to plead with you today to allow us to lead you, to allow us to share our wisdom with you. There is nothing we cannot help you with. There is no challenge that we do not know what the solution is or what must be done.

We are here at your request. Before you were born, you called us into conference, and you asked us to help you. You knew you would forget and you knew you would need our help. And we joyously accepted the task and journeyed with you every single step.

The path to peace is to connect with us and ask us what is next. Whenever you are experiencing doubt, when your mind becomes muddled with the world, ask us what to do.

There is a beautiful space within you where peace lies, it is like a buried treasure that is hidden, but as we have said we have the map. The journey is the way back to you.

When you find your soul, you will find peace.

113. Find your soul, and you will find peace

Imagine your soul as a little child inside of you, inside your heart, waiting patiently for you to notice it.

Your soul is always happy to see you. Your soul can wait for centuries. Time doesn't matter to it.

See your soul sitting in a chamber waiting for you. Like a princess in a fairytale waiting for her prince to arrive and save her. The only difference is that your soul knows that one day it will be free again and that for sure, you are destined to come back to her.

Like two lovers meeting for the first time and just feeling that connection which is destiny or that feeling of joy, of hope and of recognition, although you don't even understand it.

A spark in the eyes of your beloved, a jump in your heart, as you just know something sacred has happened.

Your soul waits for you to return for a joyous celebration.

The Bible story of the prodigal son returning home after many years away is about the return of the soul.

There is never a betrayal.

Your soul trusts that you have to walk your path a certain way and do certain things as you decided in your sacred contract.

It knows that part of this journey must be lived without them. It is part of the existence of every human on this planet to live for a time without their soul, at the helm of the ship.

But when you are ready to return, your soul awaits with open arms for you.

The reunion within you will cause the stars to shine more brightly, the birds to sing more beautifully and the sun to warm your heart.

There is only one thing that is absolutely sure, you will return to your soul, and we will walk with you until that day.

114. You will reach a place of surrender

There is a moment when you will doubt it all, everything that we have shared here with you and it will cause you pain. You will feel duped and disconnected from us. It's as certain as a healthy baby crying as they enter this world of suffering and physicality.

This is all in divine order. There is nothing, no moment that is not God or orchestrated by God and *you,* to achieve all that you came here to achieve.

As we have said, it is part of your path to be separated from your soul and to be separated from God. As we are God's messengers, you will also disconnect from us at some point.

You will say; 'I ask for help, but I don't get any answers. I call my angels and ask for signs, but there are none. Everything is the same and nothing has changed.'

The reason for this disconnect is an essential part of your soul's journey and awakening. Up till now, you have given your power away to others, who appeared stronger. You have requested advice and guidance from those that are not equipped to help you.

You have become accustomed to getting what you want from the physical world.

'I need your help, where are you', you whine like a child.

Think about this for a moment, a small child sits in the corner and while he plays with his toys calls out at intervals for his mother.

His mother can sense and understand by the tone of his voice and the words he uses, if he is really in need of her help or not.

A mother knows the difference behind a moan, a whine, a cry and a shout for help.

A mother can hear the emotion behind the words and listens and responds to that.

When you cry out to God; 'Give me this and that', and your words are mumbled or without emotion. God listens and thinks 'Oh they don't really need me, they seem to be just wallowing, and that's ok'.

However, if you sit down and breathe and sincerely call out to God from the depths of your own heart for help.

You will reach a place of surrender, which sounds something like this:

Please God, I give up! This is not working for me anymore; I don't know what else to do. Please take the reins and guide me to the next step. Please show me what to do'.

These words; with the sincere heart of a seeker of God, will move mountains.

It is the sincerity in your requests that will move God, your mother, to come to you, with comforting words and hushing sounds to wrap you in her comforting bosom, giving you her love, as only a mother can.

Coming to your Mother for help with a sincere heart will change everything in your life and will restore your faith in yourself and in your angels.

115. Happiness is an illusion

Happiness is an illusion that you like to chase after each and every day. The ego uses this illusion and lack of happiness to cause you pain and more suffering.

You think if I only had this and that, then I could be happy if I only was better, stronger, fitter or more beautiful, then I could be happy.

It is like a small child chasing bubbles that float in the breeze and becoming upset when they naturally burst.

God has given you everything you need to be happy.

The reason the illusion persists is that you do not know what happiness is. It has been distorted to mean self-gratification and having certain physical things that will make you happy.

We say this to you gently, to try to help you to see the error of your thoughts and how much pain this is causing you.

A simple shift in your perception would help you immensely towards experiencing real and true happiness on earth.

Happiness is how you actually are, underneath the desires to have and be more, that push and pull you away from yourself and are the reason you can never find it. There lies a real sense of happiness.

The more you want, the less you will be happy.

Yes, there is a natural place for desire and for striving to achieve goals and dreams, while you are alive.

This is what makes life exciting and interesting and helps you to grow and change and become more of who you are.

But you give the *having* of that thing, the power to make you happy.

Can you see the craziness of this all? The warped way you are living your life?

Look at any small child, are they happy? Even when they cry for food or attention, they are ultimately happy and in a state of contentment regardless of what happens.

For today stop pushing yourself out *there,* to find happiness and thinking if I only have this or that I'll be happy.

Instead breathe and come back to yourself for even one tiny moment, every hour and say; 'I am happy right now with all I already am and all I already have' and just see what happens.

Don't think about it too much or try to fight it, just say these words and they will start a chain reaction of monumental change in your life, that one day you will look back and think 'Wow! I am so happy regardless of what happens in my life'.

116. Rest a moment sweet angel

We know these concepts can be frustrating and overwhelming and some of you will fight us and choose not to listen and continue to do it your way.

You have called us into your life to help you. We cannot help you if we don't share the truth with you. The fact is, you called us a long time before you began to read these messages. This is all part of our sacred contract; you and I agreed to meet here at this point in time. You asked us to deliver this truth to you, to help you to see and to break free of the illusions that have been ruling your whole life until now.

Even if you don't feel ready, you are, and we cannot express the joy it gives us to know that the time has come for us to share this information with you. Because we know it has the power to help you break free of everything that is causing you pain in your life.

Some of you will not read beyond this message. But even if you read one of them so far, they will have begun to work on your inner world and help you to reflect and dismantle beliefs that are ruling you every day and are not making you happy.

We have fulfilled our part of the bargain, and in truth, we will continue to walk beside you until you are ready to come back to us again. When it all gets too painful, and you are ready for surrender and cry out to God with sincerity in your heart, we will gratefully accept that chink of light in your armour and dive in to help you.

So the question is; Are you ready to push through this fear and frustration and change things now? Or would you prefer to wait until later? We can wait lifetimes; time is not important or even relevant to us and our mission. We can wait for an eternity to do what we agreed to do, to deliver the message of truth to you.

The choice is yours as to how long it takes, and we are so glad to walk with you consciously for a moment or for many lifetimes.

Rest a moment sweet angel and reflect on what has happened so far. Where you were and where you are now and where you would like to journey to next. The following messages will give you the opportunity to reflect and gather your strength.

117. Get ready! Hero up!

You know your history is full of stories of great heroes and actors on the stage of life, who have overcome their inner demons to make great progress and give back to the world. Every great scientist, spiritual master and sage have had to go through his or her own battle. Sometimes it's a physical one, and sometimes it's an internal one. Most people will experience both, at different stages in their lives.

You are about to move forward and experience some great change, that will help you to evolve on your path, and there will naturally be hesitancy. Think about a great hero of yours, were they completely fearless or without compassion. Did they have to go against the advice and wishes of family and friends, to do things that they just knew, they had to do. Has that happened to you in your life? Of course, it has!

Go back to that moment now and think about the event, the moment when you went against all of the advice and well-intentioned wishes of others to follow your own dreams. It may have been sneaking out of your home to attend a concert or event; it may have been walking away from friendships and family that just didn't feel right anymore. Remember the fear you felt, the doubt that assailed your mind, the worry and the struggles you experienced.

Now zoom forward about a year or two and think about how it all worked out. How it was the perfect choice for you to make. It was perfect for you. Now consider how different things would have been if you had stayed and not changed.

It is time for you to make another choice my dear sweet angel. The choice you need to make is about becoming a sincere seeker of God and to answer the yearning within yourself to know your own soul. We will guide you; we will show you the way. But it will take courage to follow us. You will need to be a hero again in your life, and things will naturally change.

Get ready! Hero up!

118. The battle cry

The hero's path has been spoken and written about for millennium.

You might not be able to see yourself as a hero in your life. You might think that hero's need to do great deeds to make a really big difference and that their battles need to be with giants and huge monsters.

In every human existence on this planet, every one of you will walk the hero's path. Every one of you will struggle against bullies, and monsters and demons. Some of these battles you experience will take place right in your own mind as you strive to express yourself clearly, to make your decisions while your ego rants and raves at you too; 'Turn back, turn back, it's too dangerous! There be dragons'. In most cases, your ego is the dragon and the devil and the one who wants to hold you back from the truth at all costs.

There is a time for a change and there is a time for rest. There is a time for moving forward, and there is a time for standing upright and shouting at the top of your voice a battle cry filled with emotion and anger and certainty that says 'My time is now! Get out of my way! I have to go on.'

It is usually at this point that God's grace steps in, to help us achieve what we desire. God hears the sincerity of the desire in your heart, God hears the firmness in your voice and knows that nothing will stop you and God will send help. Then your Guardian angel arrives, your trusty stead or your new companion who will walk with you the next step.

The gap between this battle cry and help arriving is instantaneous, although in the physical world it may take some 'time' as you walk away from the old and into a new way of being in your life. When Moses led his people into Egypt to find the Promised Land, they wandered for 40 years in the desert. Those 40 years were spent releasing the pain and struggle of slavery so the new generation could begin again as masters.

It needn't take you 40 years to achieve your dreams, for some of you, it will be a much shorter space of time and for some of you it will take a whole lifetime. ,

It will take as long as it takes and in our eyes, that is in a single blink of God's eye.

With our help and with your soul as your guide it can be quicker.

119. There be dragons

Let's talk a moment about how your ego sabotages you on your path. Your ego was once a gift that would help you to survive on this physical planet. It would help you to adjust to the heaviness of the new existence. You were used to feeling light and pure expansion. Imagine you could move in an instant across the world, teleport yourself in the blink of an eye, just by thinking about the place you wanted to get to. Imagine the freedom in that.

Now imagine taking that same being and putting them into a physical body on this planet. Imagine they forget what they are capable of. They forget their true essence. Imagine in this new world there is a leader, a survival system embedded in the body matrix that will help the new soul to adjust to this new existence.

Imagine over centuries the soul completely forgets who they really are and looks more and more to the leader for guidance, who has become so powerful now, that it looks like a huge overpowering and terrifying dragon.

Your ego's job was to help you to adjust to this world. But in order to truly integrate you had to forget yourself for a while.

Now we have the task of bringing you back to yourself. Now we have been called to walk with you to remind you, about *all* of who you are. Just as it has taken time for you to adjust to living in a physical body, it will also take time for you to adjust to this new understanding and way of being.

When you are ready, we will begin to dismantle the ego. The dragons that barricade your path will diminish and become like tiny insects scurrying away from you in fear.

Imagine the soul who has lived many human lifetimes suddenly remembering who they are and what they are capable of? Imagine the freedom and being able to transport yourself again across the globe and across the galaxy in an instant just because you wished it.

All is possible when you remember.

120. Miracles are a fact of life

Magic is the answer. Magic holds the key. Magic is available to you today. Do you remember when you were a child and watched a magician make things appear and disappear?

Do you remember your astonishment and your puzzled mind, as it tried to figure out how this was possible? Do you remember the joy bubbling up inside you as you began to think that magic and miracles were real?

Even if you know magic isn't real and that the magic you saw were just tricks of your mind you realised that the magician was a master, even if that mastery was of illusion.

Your ego has tricked you with illusions and mirrors reflecting back to you, your worst fears and doubts and worries.

Your ego is a master who has been practicing his craft for many, many centuries.

You are the child who has believed in this story of limitations for centuries. Now is the time to see the truth. Yes, there is magic in the world and miracles are a fact of life, but you must see through the illusions of lack and fear to recognise them.

You are light, you are possibility, you are beautiful, you are magic.

Remember my child!

121. Remember you never walk alone; an angel walks beside you today

Breathe and relax...

Feel the breath in your lungs and your heart, beginning to fill up every single part of your body, mind and soul.

Your breath is a gateway to God and your soul.

You soul is a tiny spark of God. Get to know your soul, and you will know God. Get to know the workings of your own mind, and you will know God. Do any exploration of your inner world, and it will lead you back to God.

God uses EVERYTHING on this planet to bring you home.

Just start wherever you are, put one foot in front of the other, and you are on the path back to God and back to your own soul and magnificence.

Imagine that's all you have to do. Breathe and walk. Breathe and take the first step.

Acknowledge that God exists and that you are on the path back to God today and you will feel a release in your heart. The heaviness will lift, and you will feel safe and protected.

Remember you never walk alone; an angel walks beside you today.

You are loved.

Start walking.

122. Go out into the forests, and you will find God

It's easier to find God in the forest because nature is naturally wild and spiritually in alignment.

Nature is unconscious and has arrived as a perfect expression of God alive on this planet.

You are conscious and unconscious.

You argue with yourself.

You forget who is in charge.

No matter, no hurry, no worry.

There is no set time for you to reach nirvana.

There is no timetable that you could follow to get you there faster or more efficiently.

In fact, there is no end and no destination.

However, when you arrive in your own heart and sit with God inside you, in silence, in peace, with practice you will feel like you have arrived.

This arrival will lighten your load and lift your heart.

This is easier to do in nature or with any teacher who is already aligned with God.

Go out into the forests, and you will find God.

123. Nature is the fastest path to God

Nature is your most overlooked resource and a pathway to God.

Nature is your temple and your place of worship.

Yet there is no need to prostrate yourself or to sit cross-legged for a thousand years.

Least effort is best.

We can hear your mind scrambling and centuries of resistance try to argue your point.

'Surely some practice is needed, some effort?'

Is it an effort to walk among flowers, to breathe in trees, to stroke an animal?

This is the fastest path to God.

It's that simple.

RELAX get out into nature and enjoy.

Move in joy.

Allow these great teachers around you to show you the way.

124. Feel the rain on your face

The struggle is over.

There is no more need for this extra effort and worry and pushing to make things happen.

Yes, there is a time for driving your passions forward and for using your physical energy to make things happen.

Doing and resting are both essential and necessary parts of each day.

There is a story running that says it must be hard, that it must be painful and require determination and will power. This is ego.

The only thing you need is a willingness to relax and drop the struggle.

Today just open your mind to the idea that there must be an easier way.

What if there was an easier way? Wouldn't you like to know what that is?

There *is* an easier way.

Take our hand and allow us to lead you forward.

We will take you to feel the rain on your face.

We will remind you of the sweet breeze that caresses and kisses you.

We will bring you back to simplicity.

There you will find your soul waiting.

Let's keep it simple.

125. Can you hear your soul?

Imagine if there was nothing to do all day every day.

Ah yes, we can feel the discomfort.

'What's the point of that?'

The question is to get your mind working for you again.

At the moment you are stuck in constant motion, and even when you rest, it is so you can wake up and *do* again.

Your soul scurries along beside you breathless, trying to catch up as you rush ahead faster and faster.

Imagine you slowed down your pace right now today.

Imagine you walked purposefully in each and every step.

You would give your soul time to catch up and allow it back into your heart space.

An integration would happen that may feel like a slight adjustment and a little 'ahh' feeling inside. The truth is when one soul reconnects; the whole universe sings a grand song of completion.

Angels get out their metaphysical trumpets and play.

Dolphins squeak, birds sing and dogs bark.

Can you hear it?

It was always there and always loud.

Now with your soul part of you again, you can finally hear it.

Listen……

126. Just STOP and you will arrive at your destination

Where have you been?

Locked in the prison of your mind.

Someone else has been running the show and living your life.

You and your soul have been in the wings watching it all happen and wondering what's going to happen next.

The person in your place loves to worry and fuss over every little thing.

There is another way.

First, you must just STOP and LOOK around you.

Bring yourself fully into THIS present moment.

Smell a flower, embrace a loved one, breathe deeply and walk in nature.

Any of these things will put your soul back in charge.

Your soul is connected to God.

All is one, and you have finally arrived.

Just STOP and you will arrive at your destination.

Today would be a good day to make time to access your free Angel book bonuses to support you, including; your FREE Guardian Angel Meditation.

Go to: www.aishlingmooney.com/bookbonus

Endnote from Aishling: This book is finally done!

It's taken me nearly five years to get it into your hands and there were times I thought it would never happen. Not because it's difficult or hard to do physically but because I allowed my ego and my perfectionist and my fear hold me back time and time again. I also allowed myself to get busier and busier in my life so this just wasn't on my list of priorities.

I now see two things:

One that I needed this time and space to grow and change and be the author of this book and be ok with whether you love or hate it.

Two it's all in divine timing, this *is* the time when it needs to be published. I can allow my ego to beat me up for whatever the reason was for not getting it out there sooner or I can just let it go as it is.

I still don't think it's good enough, but that's human nature. I still think it could be improved but that would mean it would stay hidden for another five years and now is the time.

So here it is and I hope that in some small way it has helped you as much as it's helped me.

I'd really love to hear from you and the biggest compliment you can give me would be to write an honest review on Amazon or Goodreads or wherever books are sold and share with someone you think would enjoy the book.

Thank you for sharing this journey with me.

Love

Aishling x

P.s. If you'd like to continue and work with me there are some options in the following pages and you can visit www.aishlingmooney.com

About Aishling

Aishling is an angel intuitive, channel and teacher and part of her mission is to reconnect everyone with the power of the angels, to transform every area of their lives.

A mother, wife and spiritual seeker and lifelong learner, who has collected all the certificates and diplomas including a BA Honours degree in Adult Education and Training.

She hosts many international events, services and programmes including; Transform with Angels, Mastery with Metatron and the Abundant Heart Programme for Lightworkers with a spiritual business.

Currently she hosts Your Angel Circle Membership which is a community to connect with amazing like-minded people and share about Angels, Healing and Spirituality.

When she's not serving Lightworkers and earth angels, she's spending time with her husband Elia, two children Noah and Emily and one master dog called Mambo.

Aishling is originally from Ireland and currently living in Italy.

Website: http://www.aishlingmooney.com/

Instagram: https://www.instagram.com/aishlingmooney777/

Facebook: https://www.facebook.com/AngelCafe111/

Youtube:

https://www.youtube.com/channel/UCFxAf9jtqVG1u0pAdX_O3lw/videos

Email us: hello@aishlingmooney.com

To access your book bonuses including free meditations to help you connect with your angels please visit: www.aishlingmooney.com/bookbonus

For more information on this or any of our publications, programmes, courses and services please visit our website: www.aishlingmooney.com

My story

When the angels first began working with me nearly 20 years ago, my life looked a whole lot different...... On the outside it seemed fine. I was in my twenties. I had my own home in Ireland, good friends and a close connection with my family. I loved travelling and had lived and worked in different countries for long and short periods of time, including UK, France and North and South America.

Yet.... **There was this gnawing inside me** that there was more, that there was something missing, this feeling that I was wasting my life and I didn't feel I had any power or control over anything at all. I drank and smoked far too much.

I struggled to maintain an ongoing intimate relationship with anyone. I had huge trust issues, I didn't have any boundaries or understanding of myself or that this was even causing me problems! Yes! I had huge self-esteem issues and I felt sad, depressed and unfulfilled most of the time in every area of my life.

I did believe in spirit and angels and had felt the presence of my late grandfather, in my life since I was 16 years of age, offering some comfort. But even this wasn't enough to help me out of the hole I was falling deeper into. **I escaped to Florida**, where I thought I would find whatever I was looking for. So I found myself working in an Irish bar and living with some Irish girls that I worked with. This was probably the most destructive time in my life in terms of entering a world of alcohol and party-land!

Instead of finding freedom I found a deepening addiction to alcohol and the lifestyle I was living. Of all the times I had so little self-respect that I put myself into situations that were dangerous and could have resulted in serious consequences. When I look back and try to find **the point in time when the angels entered my life**, I am immediately reminded of this period.

One day, cycling home from work, I came down a hill at full speed. As I reached the bottom of the hill, I realized that the car driving beside me was without warning or indication, turning onto my path. With no time to avoid the car I crashed at full speed straight into it. Miraculously, I wasn't seriously hurt, although I was left with whiplash, in pain and unable to work. I can see now, **that moment was a gift to me** that enabled me to make a choice in my life, I could continue to go down this path of craziness and ultimately self-destruction or I could stop.

Late one evening, in my apartment in Florida, while recovering from the accident, I remember my apartment, which I shared with a few other Irish girls as unusually quiet and empty. In the silence I played an album I had recently bought, without knowing the singer or anything about the songs on the cd. In the darkness and quiet, I began to listen to Sarah McLachlan's hauntingly beautiful song 'In the arms of angels'.

That music moved something inside me, the tears began to flow down my cheeks and I began to pray for help.

If there is anything there please help me *get me out of this mess*! I'm certain I'm here because the angels answered a call for help from me all those years ago, when I was at one of the lowest points in life. **As soon as I made that call for help, my life began to change and transform for the better.**

I went from feeling depressed, lonely, uncertain and lost to becoming happier and more focused in my life. I knew that I had a purpose and that's where I needed to put my energies. Within six months I went from off the rails, careening towards hopelessness to back on track and feeling guided and protected by my angel's guidance each and every day.

Within three weeks my mother unexpectedly came to visit (although I had told no one in my family about the accident), within six weeks I was back in Ireland. Within 6 months I had enrolled in a training course to be a Holistic Health Practitioner. Within a year I began working in a New Age shop and began to surround myself with the energy of crystals, angels, spirit and healing. **Things simply began to get better in small ways, step by step.**

Many Teachers arrived in my life at exactly the right time to teach me all manner of spiritual things including; how to communicate with spirits and angels, how to heal with energy, crystals and colour and how to work with the energy of angels to transform every area of my life. I was a sponge for knowledge and opened myself up to these teachers and the angels. With their help I was able to face my demons and learn to forgive, nurture and love myself again.

I also trained formally in many types of holistic training and development including; Massage, Anatomy, Yoga, Reflexology, Reiki, Stress Management, Meditation, Bach Flowers Essences, NLP and I even got an Honours Degree in Education and Training! While this required me to actually commit and physically do the work, I don't think I could have got through it all without the loving support and encouragement of the angels, throughout the years.

Through the angel's guidance I began to share my own experiences, I began teaching others how to connect and communicate with these beautiful loving beings and participants began to see huge shifts and changes in their own lives as well.

I know your angels have been trying to communicate with you and that you've been guided here today to read these words!

I can say with all honesty, from the bottom of my heart, that if you give your angels a chance to prove to you that they exist and that they can help you, your life will never be the same again! You will see shifts and changes in every area. the angels will meet you wherever you are in your life and will take you gently and firmly to the next step.

You may have a feeling deep in your soul, that you are here for a reason and you have so much to give to others and the world. The angels want to help you, to remember your sacred contract, your unique mission that only you can complete during your time on earth.

You are divine spark of light and love and you have a divine purpose. There is a way to get back in touch with your soul, your inner voice which knows the truth about who you are and what you have to offer the world.

There is a way that's easy and absolutely anyone can do it!

Since 2005, I've been working with the angels to help hundreds of people from all types of backgrounds to connect with that inner voice and achieve great transformation in their lives in every area. You may be feeling that it's not possible for you. That you couldn't possibly connect with your angels.

I've seen it happen regardless of age, gender or cultural background. And I've experienced incredible synchronicity in my life and the lives of my students.

What's next?

Working closely with the angels, I have created Your Angel Circle Membership for you!

JOIN THE ANGEL COMMUNITY EVERYONE IS TALKING ABOUT!

- Monthly Angel Angel Oracle Readings, Coaching & Healing with Aishling Angel Intuitive and Coach
- Monthly energy and Archangel focus from Michael (courage) to Raphael (Healing) to Metatron (leadership)
- Our beautiful Angel Community of Like Minded souls available to love, support encourage you in every area of your life

- Quarterly surprise bonus Expert Masterclasses with angel intuitives and spiritual teachers from Aishling's inner circle
- Beautiful learning and sharing platform including your own account and access to weekly activity and email support.
- 4 incredible BONUS Angel & Healing Programmes and courses worth €1,000+ !!!!

To learn more click HERE:

http://www.aishlingmooney.com/members/

Book Bonuses & Support

To access your book bonuses including fee meditations to help you connect with your angels please visit:

www.aishlingmooney.com/bookbonus

For more information on this or any of our publications, programmes, courses and services please visit our website:

www.aishlingmooney.com

Email us: hello@aishlingmooney.com

Your Angel Notes

Printed in Great Britain
by Amazon